MW01259860

WHY BAD THINGS

ON'T

THINGS

HAPPEN TO

GOOD

PEOPLE

FINDING LIGHT
IN THE DARKNESS

Rabbi Shaul Rosenblatt

First edition: July 2016
Copyright © 2016: Rabbi Shaul Rosenblatt
All rights reserved

ISBN: 978-1-988022-18-5

Published by Adir Press

For more information about other publications from Adir Press,
visit *www.AdirPress.com* Or to discuss publishing *your* material,
email *submissions@AdirPress.com*

In Loving Memory of
Malcolm Yardley
ז״ל

משה בן אברהם

1933—2016

Beloved husband, father and grandfather

Malcolm was devoted to his wife, Gloria
who was also his best friend. He loved his children deeply and
was always available for thoughtful advice and time together.

Much like the author, he was worldly and articulate and loved
the exchange of meaningful ideas with people around him.

But perhaps more than anything, he will be remembered
for his sense of humor. Well-liked by all, Malcolm was known
for his contagious laughter, the jokes and comical
stories that would give you a welcome lift and
always bring a smile to your face.

Dedicated by his loving family, wife Gloria,
sons Avi and Julian, daughters-in-law Debra and Rowena,
and grandchildren Leib, Shira, Shoshana, Nechama,
Asher, Yair, Joshua, James and Danielle

Rabbi Yitzchak Berkovits
Sanhedria HaMurchevet 113/27
Jerusalem, Israel 97707
02-5813847

יצחק שמואל הלוי ברקוביץ
ראש רשת הכוללים לינת הצדק
סנהדרי׳ה המורחבת 113/27
ירושלם ת״ו

ירושלם חי׳ו ח׳ בכה חח תמשי׳ז

    This is not just another book on Jewish thought or a self-help manual for dealing with suffering. Nor is it a presentation marking the culmination of extensive research and creative thinking on a topic that baffles so many. This work is a window into the heart and mind of a very special person, who became only greater through suffering and tragedy.

    I first got to know Rav Shaul Rosenblatt as a brilliant student some three decades ago. He was blessed with a superb analytical mind and a passion for truth. Years ago he could have composed an academic survey of the various rational explanations for why people suffer. Divine Providence and Rav Shaul's intelligent, responsible and mature manner in dealing with challenge, developed within him an inner strength, a depth of feeling and intense clarity. He has undoubtedly earned for himself the credentials as an authentic spokesman for the Torah approach in confronting pain.

    I am sure this book will be of assistance to so many of our people who are faced with seemingly unsurmountable challenges, and can breathe new life into those who have succumbed to despair.

    May HaShem teach us all to feel close to Him through joy, and afford the author a happy, healthy meaningful life sharing of his wisdom with so many of our brethren.

בברכה,

יצחק ברקוביץ

The Office of   PO Box 72007   T +44 (0)20 7286 6391
RABBI SACKS   London   info@rabbisacks.org
NW6 6RW   www.rabbisacks.org

Rabbi Shaul Rosenblatt has written a deeply personal and profoundly moving account of what it is to wrestle with suffering and find meaning in a world fraught with pain.

This is a work of courage and faith that will give courage and faith to those who read it and absorb its hope-filled message.

Rabbi Lord Jonathan Sacks
March 2016 – Adar II 5776

Letter of Approbation from
Rabbi Dr. Akiva Tatz

This book deals with the age-old question of why bad things happen to good people, from a deeply personal perspective. Rabbi Shaul Rosenblatt has been there, experienced the depths of personal loss, and shows us how to live through and beyond such pain in a genuine and even inspiring way. Reading his story provides a sensitive guide to those dealing with suffering who are open to transforming their experience.

A. Tatz

יחיאל מיכל טווערסקי

כאאמו"ר הרה"צ כמוהר"ר יעקב ישראל זצללה"ה מהאָרנאָסטייפאָל

Rabbi Michel Twerski

18 Adar II, 5776

To Bnai Yisroel Everywhere :

   Although I rarely have occasion to peruse an entire manuscript, Rabbi Shaul Rosenblatt's, 'Why Bad Things Don't Happen to Good People', proved to be an exception to the rule. Page after page, it held my interest, to the extent that, despite its painful topic, I found it hard to put down. Rabbi Rosenblatt offers thoughtful suggestions, personal experiences, compelling examples and inspired metaphors to help us navigate the turbulent rapids of pain and bereavement. Building on principles of "Emunah" and " Bitochon", he defines the parameters of "Bechirah" with such clarity and poignance that he enables us to go beyond the sheer tolerance of suffering, to actually grow taller from it. While we all pray that Hashem not test us, since life rarely spares anyone the luxury of no "nisyonos", we need the insightful, straightforward wisdom offered in this book, to provide us the perspective and direction to transcend and transform our pain to a personal triumph. I have every confidence that 'Why Bad Things Don't Happen to Good People'.will be well received, and offer my humble blessings that the future will bring Rabbi Rosenblatt and all of Klal Yisroel, only Bracha, Hatzlacha and Simcha, until the coming of Moshiach Tzidkeinu, speedily in our time.

With every good wish, I am
Sincerely,

Rabbi Michel Twerski

LETTER OF APPROBATION

International

FOUNDER & DEAN
Rabbi Noah Weinberg

DAN FAMILY OF CANADA
WORLD CENTER
Jerusalem, Israel

AISH PROGRAMS
Aish.com
Aishaudio.com
Aish on Campus
Aish Productions
Discovery Production
EYAHT
Essentials
Executive Learning Center
Hasbara Fellowships
HonestReporting
Jerusalem Fellowships
Jerusalem Partners
JEWEL
Jewish Family Institute
Project Chazon
Russian Program
SpeedDating®
Spanish Division
The Jerusalem Fund
Yeshivat Aish HaTorah

AISH BRANCHES
Ashdod, Israel
Baltimore
Bat Yam, Israel
Birmingham, UK
Boston
Cleveland
Denver
Detroit
Essex, UK
Jerusalem, Israel
Johannesburg, SA
Kiev, Ukraine
Las Vegas
Livingston, NJ
London
Los Angeles
Manchester, UK
Melbourne, Australia
New York
Petach Tikva, Israel
Philadelphia
Santiago, Chile
Sao Paulo, Brazil
Scottsdale, AZ
Seattle
South Florida
St. Louis
Toronto
Washington, DC
Winnipeg, CA

Jerusalem
June 13, 2006

Shaul Rosenblatt has written a book that is personal, deeply moving, and deeply wise. It is extremely enjoyable and readable while being profoundly insightful. I think it will be greatly meaningful and helpful to anyone grappling with life's challenges.

I highly recommend for everyone to read this book.

Rabbi Noah Weinberg

American Friends of Yeshiva Aish HaTorah, Inc.
400 South Lake Drive • Lakewood, NJ 08701-3167 • Tel: 732-364-6683 • Fax: 732-875-0576 • Email: info@aish.com
Tax ID# (EIN): 51-0243498 • Exemption granted pursuant to section 501(c)(3) of the Internal Revenue Code

For my late wife, Elana

*Thank you
for filling my world with light.*

And for Chana, *lhbcl'c*

*Thank you for making my life brighter
than I could have ever dreamed possible.*

Contents

Publisher's Preface

Why Bad Things Don't Happen to Good People is not a book of suffering; it is a book of growth. Although the author, Rabbi Shaul Rosenblatt undoubtedly suffered as a result of losing his wife after a difficult illness, ultimately, Rabbi Rosenblatt *grew* from his experiences. It is as a direct result of this growth that "Bad Things Don't Happen to Good People" was written.

Over a period of fifteen years, the book you are about to read was written, and re-written many times. Not only is this apparent from the quality of writing, but throughout this book we are enjoined to appreciate deep concepts and philosophical thoughts that have taken years to grasp and develop. Yet, this is far from a heavy philosophical book that must be read several times in order to gain a simple understanding; it is a book which is easily understood and quite literally life-changing. It is for *this* reason that it should be read several times!

It has been a privilege to have been involved in the editing and publication of "Why Bad Things Don't Happen to Good People." Besides the content, I was inspired by Rabbi Rosenblatt's honest approach to life, and was humbled by his unwillingness to write even one word that he doesn't fully understand or agree with.

It is my fervent prayer that people learn from this book and grow from its message, and come to appreciate life's challenges. *B'ezras Hashem* this book will help those who are suffering as well as those who struggle with the question of Hashem's providence in the world.

May the Jewish People know no more suffering, and may we only hear *b'soros tovos*.

Rabbi Moshe Kormornick
Adir Press

Preface

Why Bad Things Don't Happen to Good People is about the understanding I developed — both together with my late wife Elana, *z"l*, and subsequently, alone — that helped us deal with incredibly challenging circumstances. I am hoping that the lessons I learned will be of help to others who are facing difficulty. We all go through pain in our lives. No one is exempt. What makes some people different from others is how they rise to the challenge of their pain. I hope to share some ideas that the reader may find of value.

Rabbi Shaul Rosenblatt

Acknowledgements

Firstly, a big thank you to Rabbi Moishe Kormornick of Adir Press who has encouraged and supported me throughout this endeavor. This book is so much better because of his input.

Many people have helped me to make this book possible. I would like to express my appreciation to:

My rebbe, Rabbi Noah Weinberg, of blessed memory, who taught me the foundations of everything I know. Hardly a day goes by when I do not miss your wisdom.

Rebbetzen Dena Weinberg, whose *tznius* will not allow me to say too much, but if I did, I probably could not say enough.

My parents, who gave me life, a loving family and a warm home from which to build my own.

Joanne and Irwin Asher, thank you for the beautiful and precious woman who graced and blessed my life for twelve years.

Rabbi Yissachar and Esther Granitsky, thank you for the beautiful and precious woman who graces and blesses my life today.

Family, friends and community who have all been so incredibly supportive along the way.

Elana, who taught me how to love, how to be loved and, above all, how to love God. Words simply cannot express the debt of gratitude that I owe you. This book is yours, not mine.

And, of course, to my wise wife Chana, who has encouraged me, supported me and advised me throughout. If I have anything to offer, it is ONLY because of you. You picked us up when we were lost and helped us find ourselves again.

Thank you *Hashem* for blessing me with the republishing of this book.

Introduction

The question addressed by this book: why bad things happen to good people, is perhaps the oldest philosophical question posed by mankind. It is as relevant and poignant to us today as it has ever been. Let me lay out the question simply as a starting point for my discourse.

It is a question predicated by Monotheism. Only if you believe in One God does the question even begin.

For the atheist, why should bad things not happen to good people? A human being is a random collection of atoms in the same fashion as a carrot. Any difference in value is conceived, but not actual. So there should be no philosophical difference between the random destruction of a carrot and the random destruction of a human being, whether he is good or not. And the same would be true of a million carrots destroyed in a tsunami and a million human beings. Both situations are simply atoms in one form being shifted, via external causes, to another form. It is one of the conveniences of Atheism not to have to be concerned by such questions.

And for a polytheist, there is no question either. Why do bad things happen to good people? Because you worshipped the wrong god today. Or you worshipped the right one but in the wrong way. In Polytheism, there is no concept of the gods representing values in any way. They are almost as human as we are. They certainly do not have higher principles that they adhere to, because there is no room for higher principles without a Supreme, Infinite Being — something that is distinctly absent in the philosophy of Polytheism. (And if a Supreme Being does exist in a particular form of Polytheism, then that religion is Monotheism in a different guise)

The question can only possibly arise once it is predicated by a God Who is outside of time and space, and hence absolute. Such a God must, by definition, be absolutely 'good' and absolutely 'just.' And, as such, when we look at a world of pain and suffering, we wonder how

He can be good. And more so, when we see a world in which it is the good that suffer, we wonder further how He can be just also.

So the question of 'why bad things happen to good people', has existed for as long as Monotheism has existed. And historically, there have been many who have rejected the concept of Monotheism based on this question alone.

There is, of course, a secondary question, the inverse of the first. Why do good things happen to bad people? Whilst I do touch on this question, I don't address it directly. This is for two reasons. Firstly, in my experience it is a question of much less pressing concern for most people. It might be of philosophical interest, but it certainly does not seem to arouse the intense passion of the first question. And secondly, I do believe that the basis for the answer to this question is found in the ideas that I bring to answer its twin.

I have purposely left my story to the end (Part Two), as my primary goal is that this be a book of Jewish philosophy, not a personal account. However, my story certainly has a bearing on the question that I aim to answer and hence I have included it later on in the book. If you wish to read it first, that order would be no less logical than the order I have chosen.

If you do not, let me give a brief synopsis as I do often refer to it in the body of the book.

In 1998, my wife and soul mate, Elana Golda was diagnosed with breast cancer. It was stage four from the outset — barring miracles, a death sentence. She responded to her illness with acceptance, with fortitude, above all with grace and a deep sense of gratitude towards God. Three years later, she passed away peacefully in the quiet of our own living room, surrounded by those who loved her most. She left me so many blessings, not least of all four beautiful and precious children.

I learned so much from those three years — most of which I learned directly from you, Elana. And so much since, as a result. You were my teacher, my guide and my light through the most challenging period of my life. This book should have been written by you, not me. But God had other plans and it is me who remains to write, while your soul was called back to His better and more beautiful world. May God bless you, Elana. I could never repay you for the extent to which you have blessed me.

Part One

Why Bad Things Don't Happen to Good People

Chapter 1
Pain and Suffering

T he book of Job is surely the most shocking book of the Bible.
Job is a righteous man — there is "no one like Him on earth;
pure, straight, God-fearing, and does no evil" *(Job 1:8)*. He is
wealthy, accomplished, respected, and the father of ten children.

God decides to test Job. And it's not a stubbing-one's-toe type of
test. In one fell swoop, his children die and his wealth is completely
obliterated.

"Naked I left my mother's womb and naked shall I return. God
gave and God took back. May the name of God be blessed" (ibid
1:21). This is Job's answer. If ever there was a noble and dignified
response to adversity, this is surely it. It seems as though Job's faith is
unshakable.

Now God ups the stakes and covers Job's entire body with horribly
painful blisters. Once again, his response is incredible. His wife asks
why he is still blessing God when God has put him through all this,
and he says to her, "We have accepted the good from God, shall we
not also accept the bad from Him?" (ibid 2:10).

His three friends come to visit him and are stunned by what they
see has happened. They are left speechless. They sit with Job for seven
days without a single word passing between them.

At the end of the seven days, for no apparent reason, Job snaps.
A more drastic turnaround could not be imagined. He rants and he
raves. He complains and he curses. He says, "Why did I not die in
my mother's womb?" and "Never did I feel secure, never quiet, never
at peace and now torment?" (ibid. 3:10 and 3:25). Later on, he says,
"Even if I were to call and He [God] were to answer me, I don't believe
He would listen to my voice. For He has shattered me in a tempest for
no good reason" (ibid., 9:16–17). "I am disgusted with my life" (ibid.

9:21). "My days are so few — leave me alone, distance yourself from me so that I can find some respite. Before I depart, never to return, to a land of gloom and of death's shadow, a land darkened by the darkness of death's shadow and chaos — its brightest spots grim darkness" (ibid. 10:20–22). "His anger slashed me — He hates me" (ibid. 16:9).

I could go on; Job certainly does. Within moments, he has transformed from a righteous and holy man, accepting of God's challenges, into an embittered existentialist philosopher.

His friends try to comfort him. And these are no ordinary friends. All are prophets, men of spiritual greatness. Each tries to tell him of God's goodness and ultimate justice. And to each, Job's arguments back are scathing, sarcastic, and bitter. It's hard to believe that we are listening to the same man.

The oral tradition itself seems to struggle with the book of Job. On the question of when he lived, there are no less than fifteen different opinions — more than on any other topic in the Talmud. I once asked my teacher, Rabbi Weinberg of blessed memory, how he understands the message of the book. He said that in his opinion, Job is certainly a good man. He is a righteous man, a man who trusts in God. But the bottom line is that adversity is hard for anyone. It's not easy to lose all your property and retain perspective, to lose all your children and keep smiling. It's not easy to go through hardship and continue to bless God. Facing hardship is not easy for even the greatest of human beings. Anyone can crack under pressure — as did Job.

To me, this is an incredibly encouraging message. Only God is perfect. We are mere human beings. And when we go through hardship — as we all do — it can be overwhelming. We may well respond with frustration, bitterness, and even anger and resentment towards God. *And that's okay.*

God understands. He created us as human beings and, as such, He knows our human frailties better than anyone. So as much as God does get frustrated, so to speak, with Job at the same time, God still comes to him in the end of the book and His soliloquies are the longest in the Bible, spoken by God directly. God takes the time to ease Job's troubled heart and in the end, God's love and patience penetrate. Job rants and raves against God; God takes it all from him and then comforts him.

I don't know how to emphasize this point enough. I'm going to write a lot about how to go through hardship with grace, how to have a healthy attitude towards adversity. But throughout it all, this will be my underlying message. We're human. We can hear the most wonderful and uplifting ideas about what hardship means and how to grow from it, but hardship will still be…hard, and sometimes we will feel overwhelmed by that pain. If a man such as Job is allowed to lose it for a little while, then so is any one of us.

I'm not suggesting that we do! It's certainly going to be a better experience if a person remains strong and steadfast in the face of challenge. However, I'm saying that we're God's children and if suffering makes us angry at Him, He understands that it's not easy and loves us no less for it.

Moshe

There's a man who I knew in Jerusalem many years ago and he was one of the happiest people I've ever met. With tremendous concentration, he could move his right hand a tiny amount, but apart from that, he was paralyzed from the neck down. I will call him Moshe.

Back in the 60s, Moshe was in his twenties and studying at a college in the U.S. He was good looking, athletic, from a relatively affluent family, and a straight "A" student. By the standards of his society, he had it all.

Then the race riots began. A black man walked onto his campus looking to shoot a white man; no one in particular, as long as he was white. Moshe was the first man he came across and he shot Moshe in the neck.

Moshe was in a coma for a time, and when he finally came to, he was told that he would be paralyzed for the rest of his life.

Moshe says that his first response was, *how could this happen to me?* He thought about this for a long time, and a further question developed.

Now that he did not have the use of his arms or legs, what was it that would make life worth living?

His thoughts flowed further. And when he *had* had the use of his arms and legs, had that made life worth living? What had he been living for up until this point? Had he ever considered what life was about in the first place? It was certainly not about having arms and legs. It's just that when he had arms and legs he had enough distractions not to have to worry about what life was about.

But now that they were useless, he felt a need to consider what he was living for.

More thoughts occurred to him.

If he had not been paralyzed, would he have ever stopped and thought about what he was living for? Almost certainly not. So what is worse, he asked himself — for a person to go through his whole life without the use of his arms and legs; or for a person to go through his whole life with no idea what he is living for? Given the choice, he said to himself, he would take the former.

Eventually Moshe became an Orthodox Jew and moved to Jerusalem. He married a woman who was totally devoted to him and welcomed many guests to his table every *Shabbos*. I was fortunate to be one of them. During the time I spent there, when I was single, I found his home full of joy. His disability did not impede his happiness. In fact, in some strange way, it enhanced it.

I recall that when we sang Jewish songs at his home, he would ask two of us to lift him onto his feet. Although he could not move his legs, with great difficulty he could somehow hold his own weight on his legs with us supporting him. Gradually, he would manage to use the muscles in his neck in order to sway his body back and forth as we sang, dancing to the rhythm of the music. The look on his face when he was able to do that was nothing less than ecstatic. Joy burned inside of him.

At the time it was always difficult for me to comprehend how someone who was so clearly good should be given such a test. Why did bad things happen to good people like Moshe? Equally, however, it was difficult for me to understand how he could find such happiness in the midst of such tragedy.

That was before Elana passed away. Nowadays, the answers to those questions seem obvious to me.

Why Do Bad Things Happen to Good People

T he question is one that Elana and I struggled with over the difficult years of her illness. Eventually, we found an answer that satisfied us both. And its simplicity always amazed me. It needs no drum rolls or introduction. The answer is simply this:

Bad things do not happen to good people.

And bad things don't happen to bad people either. Bad things simply don't 'happen.' I'm not playing with words. I'm merely using, as I'll explain, the most meaningful definitions available.

The question of why bad things happen is not a new one — it's as old as Judaism itself and is raised in many, many places.

"It is not in our hands — neither the suffering of the righteous nor the comfort of the wicked," says Rabbi Yannai *(Ethics of the Fathers 4:15).*

How can we possibly understand, in the context of a loving Father in Heaven, people dying young, parents losing children, disease, starvation, wars, gas chambers, and crematoria? It just doesn't seem to work.

I believe that much of our difficulty in dealing with bad things happening comes from a definition of bad that is entirely inconsistent with Judaism's definition.

I would imagine that for most people, the working definition of 'bad' in the context of the question 'why do *bad* things happen to good people' is pain. Be it the pain someone goes through while dying from a horrible disease, the pain of someone like Elana, knowing she will never dance at her children's weddings, or the pain of children starving in Africa or the Warsaw Ghetto. It's the pain involved in these situations that makes us judge them as bad. If no one in the Holocaust went through any pain — if they were gently put to sleep without any knowledge of what was happening — we would still see it as a horrible thing, but it would not invoke the feeling of overwhelming and unbearable pain that it does.

Maybe take a few moments to consider this before moving on.

If pain is to be in any way linked with our definition of bad — be it emotional, physical, or spiritual pain — then the question of why bad things happen is fairly well unanswerable. Because pain happens to every human being, righteous or evil, throughout most of their lives, and if pain in and of itself is bad, then God has clearly made a world that is just filled with 'bad.'

But before we come to such a conclusion, let's examine our assumptions for a moment. Is pain necessarily bad?

Daniel

I once had a guest, Daniel, over for dinner. He was in the process of recovering from a coma that he had been in for two years, due to massive brain hemorrhaging during an operation. He had still not regained his sense of touch and so could not feel anything anywhere in his body.

As a little boy, I had heard about people like Daniel, who have no sense of touch. And I was incredibly jealous. If only it happened to me, I used to think, I would never feel pain again in my life — no painful injections, no dentist's drill, no pain when I fall off my bike. If only I could have no sense of touch, life would be wonderful. It was only as an adult that I realized how disastrous this would actually be and it was brought home to me very clearly when Daniel came for dinner.

I had noticed that he had been nervous about eating during dinner, but it was only when I gave him a cup of tea for dessert that I realized why. He asked one of our children to test it for him and see how hot it was. Without being able to feel, he was unable to judge temperature and he could very easily drink boiling hot tea, and scald his mouth and throat, without even realizing that he was doing so. With his early warning system of pain gone, he could be destroying his body without noticing. Were he to tread on a piece of glass, for example, he could continue walking without knowing that he was tearing his foot to shreds. Yes, he felt no pain, but because of that, he could not even drink a cup of tea without someone else's help.

Physical pain is clearly something necessary for us and very beneficial.

Cancer is another obvious example. A lack of pain in its early stages is one of the main reasons why it is such a deadly disease. Were cancer to be painful immediately, very few people would actually die from it. If cancer could be felt the moment it began, doctors could respond to it at a very early stage. They could cut it out before it had a chance to spread to other parts of the body. Unfortunately, this is not the case. Rarely is the disease detected by the person feeling pain. Our doctor told us that Elana's cancer had certainly existed for months, and possibly even years, before she detected it. Cancer is deadly precisely because it begins painlessly.

In the case of cancer, as with Daniel, it is the lack of pain that is the 'bad' thing — and a very 'bad' thing at that. Pain would actually be a 'good' thing in these circumstances.

Clearly, pain is a complex phenomenon. To merely label it as 'bad' is to grossly oversimplify the matter.

A Broken Leg

To expand this a little further, let's imagine that someone is walking down the street, minding his own business — maybe even on the way to do a good deed — and a car, driven by someone who is drunk, mounts the curb and runs him over. His leg is broken in four places and he requires an immediate operation, with six weeks recovery in the hospital afterwards.

Good or bad?

Obviously it's bad, you say. And you will wonder why such a 'bad' thing happened to a person who was on his way to do a good deed.

Yet, if we jump so quickly to this conclusion, we are again making the mistake of oversimplification.

Let's say the operation goes well and our patient is recuperating in a hospital ward. The next day, he meets a lovely young lady in the same ward. She is also going to be in the hospital for a few weeks. They start talking. They don't get on so well at first, but as time goes by they begin to like each other. After all, if you talk to someone for hours each day, you will eventually find something to like about them. Their attraction grows over time. They find that they have many shared interests. They are from similar backgrounds and have the same life goals. Once out of the hospital, they start going out. After a short while, they become engaged. Eventually, they marry and live happily ever after.

Now, let's ask this man, fifty years later, as he sits with his great-grand-children on his lap at his golden wedding anniversary, whether it was a good or bad thing that the car ran him over on that fateful day. Looking back, he would in no way consider it a bad thing. Painful, yes, but it was pain that brought an incredible amount of goodness in its wake. If you were to offer him the opportunity to go back in time and not be hit by that car, he would not dream of taking it.

This is an example of short term adversity that brings long term results. The pain of his broken leg disappeared after a few weeks. The goodness of his marriage to the woman he met in the hospital was eternal.

Once again, pain is not always 'bad.'

Elana always used to remind me that life is like a jigsaw puzzle. Sometimes you pick up a piece and it looks like it's not going to fit. It just doesn't look like it belongs in this jigsaw. Maybe the manufacturer accidentally included a piece from another puzzle. You put it aside and start to put the puzzle together. As the picture in the puzzle grows, it begins to dawn on you that this strange piece might actually have its place. More pieces fit into place and you see clearly now that this piece was in the right box. When you are almost done, you know exactly where this piece is going to go. And finally, the puzzle is complete, apart from this one piece. When you put this seemingly defective piece in its correct position, it is just what is necessary to make the puzzle complete and perfect. Without it, the puzzle would not work.

So too in life, Elana would say, there are pieces thrown our way that seem like they should not be there. Surely this is not meant to happen in my life? Surely this is not right for me? As life develops and time goes on, we start to see that what happened might just have its place in the bigger picture of life. Eventually, we come to realize that not only does this have its place, it is a beautiful part of the puzzle, entirely necessary to make the story of life complete and perfect. It just requires some patience. Thirteen years after losing Elana, I can say with certainty that God knew exactly what He was doing with this piece of the puzzle in my life. It was a painful and challenging experience – but it has fit just right and I would not have wanted it any other way.

Now you may ask at this point, 'That's fine for you to say, but you are not the only one who was affected by her passing away.' How can you talk for others? I do directly address these issues later in the book, but I will give a brief response here:

I can speak for Elana — because as every religious Jew knows, she is in a better place and she is happy. And I can speak for my children — not only do I clearly see the goodness in their lives but I have had discussions with every one of them and I can confidently say that each one of them sees how this puzzle piece fits perfectly into their own lives. But, yes, there are those for whom I cannot speak directly. However, I believe that my approach in this book is relevant for anyone going through pain in whatever context, and that will ultimately be my answer for others as well as for myself.

Defining "Bad"

I hope that by now it's obvious that 'pain' is not useful as a definition for 'bad.' Perhaps some pain really is bad (though we as yet have no examples of that type of pain), but certainly not all pain is bad. And so we are going to have to refine our definition.

At this point, we might be tempted to redefine bad as "pain that brings no positive results." But then it would be impossible for us to ever decide whether something was good or bad. For who is to say what good might come in ten years or twenty, or perhaps not even in this world, but in the next one? Such a definition of bad would be of no use to us whatsoever. Until we were fully aware of the ramifi-cations of any event — in both this world and the next — we could not make a judgment that it was 'bad' (or 'good' for that matter). To define 'bad' in this way would be tantamount to having no definition of 'bad' whatsoever.

Because of this, the best we can say is: Pain, in and of itself, is fairly neutral. It's not pleasant, it's not comfortable, it's not nice, but it's also neither bad nor good.

Why God might make something painful or create the entire con-cept of pain in the first place are issues that I will deal with later, but suffice to suggest at this point: pain has no meaningful role in trying to define 'bad.'

The Jewish Definition

The Jewish People have a very different definition of bad — and based on this definition, nothing bad ever really 'happens' in this world.

The easiest way to define 'bad' is by first defining 'good'.

"Good" is something that enables you to become more Godly. And conversely, "bad" is something that makes you a less Godly person. Torah is good. *Mitzvos, good deeds*, are good. God Himself is good. And conversely, moving away from God — the source and root of all goodness — is bad.

Put a different way, good is that which leads us towards self-perfec-tion; that which enables us to become the great human beings we are capable of becoming; that which helps us to find the closeness to God that is available to us. Bad is that which takes us away from God, that which hinders us from achieving our potential.

These are the Jewish definitions and the ones I will generally use for the rest of this book. It's worth taking just a few minutes to con-sider the implications of these definitions before reading any further.

Let's take a look at pain in the context of these definitions.

As a rule, does pain and difficulty in life make it easier or harder to rise spiritually? In truth, the answer is probably neither. We have freewill and we make our own choices in life. But in looking at the world, it does seem to me that great people in history have more often than not found their greatness through adversity. Greatness is not usually found among those who spend their days lying on beaches and sailing around the world in million-dollar yachts. Greatness is much more often found among those who face adversity head on and overcome it. Those who achieve their true potential are usually those who struggle through difficult situations and build their character in the process. The Talmud tells us, "Be careful of the children of the poor, for from them comes Torah" *(Nedarim 81a)*.

Far from being a hindrance, hardship is actually something that can be of great value. If 'good' is something that has the potential to help us come closer to God, then hardship is certainly good.

Let's revisit the man with the broken leg — even without knowing that he ended up meeting his future wife due to it. Let's look at it as a plain and simple broken leg; seemingly nothing more gained other than pain and temporary disability. Is that good or bad?

The Jewish answer is still, of course, neither. But now there is something to add.

It could be good, or it could be bad. It all depends on what this man does with it. A broken leg can make him angry and upset and take him away from God. Or the pain can help him to put aside some of his pettiness and bring him closer to God.

The choice is his.

The broken leg is certainly a challenge — but if our friend rises to the challenge and overcomes it, he will lift himself to a Godlier realm. It is not good or bad. It is, however, a significant opportunity for good — should he choose for it to be so. And if he does, then he will look back fifty years later and say that yes, it was wonderful that he met his wife through his broken leg, but even more wonderfully, the broken leg enabled him to employ his freewill to lift himself to new levels of personal greatness.

There is nothing — absolutely nothing — that happens to us in this world that is good or bad. All is completely neutral.

Of course, I am talking here from the human perspective. Events come at us neutrally and we make of them what we will. But from the perspective of God, the Being that is *only* good, it is with a higher purpose, and hence is a more ultimate good that the events we experience are neutral to us. In other words, God's will is that we should experience neutral events in this world in order that we have the ability to choose. The system is 'good', even when the details are 'not'. *Our world can be good or our world can be bad*, and God wants us to be the sole arbiters of that for ourselves. The fact that the neutrality of events enables our freewill makes that neutrality itself a good thing. For us human beings, events are neutral. For God, a system of neutral events is an ultimate good. The result of this is that every circumstance has the potential to lift us to a greater level of goodness — or direct us away from God. Everything has the potential to be good and everything has the potential to be bad. Our reaction to what happens is the deciding factor. 'Bad' things don't happen to good people. But neither do 'good' things. Things happen that could be either more or less painful. But they are not inherently good or bad. We human beings are the sole arbiters as to whether that which occurs in our lives will ultimately be good or bad.

Elana and I made a decision when she first became ill. We didn't have a choice as to whether or not she would have cancer. But we did have a choice as to how we would respond to that cancer. We knew that we could allow ourselves to despair, that we could hide ourselves away from the world and accept our fate. Or we could decide to be happy with the goodness that we had. We could make sure we enjoyed our time with each other and our children and enjoyed our lives in general. We knew that we could grow closer to God at this time or we could move further away — and, whilst we were human and there would be times that we would lose perspective, nevertheless that choice was within our hands much of the time.

The *Mishnah*, Jewish Oral Tradition, tells us that Abraham was tested with ten tests. Each one was given to him in order to show how much God loved him *(Ethics of the Fathers 5:3)*. At first glance this seems strange. Here's how you show you love someone? Firstly, you have him thrown into a furnace. Then, you tell him to pack his bags and move to a foreign country. When he obeys, you bring a famine to this country. And then, when he travels to find food, you have the ruler of the next place abduct his wife. Abraham gets her back and returns to his ordained place of residence, only to find that his nephew has been kidnapped by four powerful kings. He manages to release him and is then commanded to kill his only son. Upon his return, having overcome the greatest challenge of his life, he finds that his wife died from shock and he is forced to pay an exorbitant sum for an inferior burial plot in a land that God has already promised him as an inheritance. And all of this shows God's love for Abraham?!

Yes! This is precisely God's love. Because through these challenges, Abraham was able to come closer to God. He fulfilled his potential and became the great human being we know of, founder of the nation that has taught Monotheism to the world. The pain was relatively short-lived. The results were eternal. Abraham sits in his place in eternity, not in spite of his hardships, but because of them. His pain is gone. His greatness remains forever.

And so, I ask you to consider — what are you in this world for? To be comfortable? To avoid pain? To live out seventy or eighty years of life with the least challenge possible? If this is your aim, then many 'bad' things will happen along the way — because this is a world of pain and pain is antithetical to all that you are living for. If, however, you believe, as I do, that we are here to lift ourselves into Godliness, to grow and to strive towards self-perfection and spiritual enlightenment then all that happens to us is a golden opportunity — and the more challenging it is, the greater that opportunity. The *Mishnah* tells us that "according to the difficulty is the reward" *(Ethics of the Fathers 5:23)*. The level of difficulty in a situation defines the level of potential for Godliness. Of course, we don't go looking for hardship in life, but when it comes, we are not afraid of it; far from it, we embrace it as an opportunity to strive towards perfection.

The Rabbis take this to its logical extreme. They say *(Eruchin 16b)* that if someone has had no challenges for forty days, he has "acquired his world." This means that God is no longer testing him, no longer giving him the opportunity to grow. God has given up on him ever becoming anything more than he is right now, because he has shown that he is not interested in growing. Instead, God has simply chosen to let him live out his days in this world without attaining deeper levels of perfection. The Rabbis tell us *(Makkos 10b)* that, "God leads us in the way that we wish to go." He doesn't force us, He responds to our choices. This person has chosen to have no interest in spiritual development, God responds by leading him along this road – and hence gives him no challenges.

If I've done my job well, you may now raise the question of why it is then that some people whom we would consider 'bad' also have hard times. I would respond to this with a few points. Firstly, how are you judging a bad person? Can you look into the truth of his soul? Can you judge him in the context of his challenges or just by the superficiality that you see? Secondly, though, how are you judging hard times? As I've said before, some people go through difficult times and do fine, whilst others are overwhelmed by a toothache. Putting those two ideas together, I believe the true answer to this question is that humans choosing and God responding in real time is such a complex and constantly fluctuating system that it is impossible for a person to look at the current details of someone's life, which are miniscule in the grand scheme of their total existence, as well as the lives of all of their past and future generations, and figure out what's really going on. We can understand some broad principles, many of which I'm trying to put across in this book, but there is a point at which our understanding must break down because our ability to grasp the enormity of the system is ultimately very limited. We see a small scene within a vast tapestry. Only God is privy to the whole picture. Hence, only God is able to truly judge.

Coming back, however, a life free of challenge might sound great on some level, but it is not something that interests us as Jews. We may not like them, and we certainly do not ask for them, but we do actually want the challenges that will help us achieve our potential.

At the height of Elana's illness, and at the times of my deepest pain afterwards, this is what I kept reminding myself. I put signs up all around my house saying, "We are in this world to use our freewill to get closer to God — nothing else." We all have different scenarios in which we are placed — some more painful, some less. But it is all directed towards the same end. Specific circumstances merely give us a context in which to use our freewill to lift ourselves towards Godliness. Borrowing from Shakespeare, I would think of every human being as acting in a giant play — a play that generally lasts seventy or so years — and a play in which there will be great drama and tragedy, plenty of comedy too. Each of our plays has a different script, a different challenge. The acts and scenes may be different, but the underlying plot is the same for all seven billion of us. We are charged with the mission of using our freewill and lifting ourselves closer to God. Circumstances may be fluid, but challenge is a constant — the purpose behind all events in life!

My friends, take it from me, pain passes. All pain passes. If not in this world, then certainly in the next. A cut finger might take a few minutes, a headache an hour, a stomachache a day, a sprained ankle a week, a broken leg a month, and a broken heart may even take a lifetime. But no pain will carry through to the World of Truth. It is the decisions we make, the way we choose to face that challenge and transcend that pain, which will remain with us for eternity. These decisions, and these decisions alone, are the purpose of our years in this world.

Reb Zusha

The story is told of some *Chassidim*, a sect of Orthodox Jews, who went to their Rebbe to ask why bad things happen to good people. His response was simple: "Go visit Reb Zusha of Anipoli."

The *Chassidim* had heard about Reb Zusha's poverty, suffering, illnesses and difficult life and were eager to hear what the righteous Reb Zusha had to say. He could talk to them from personal experience. He had been through real pain in his life. He was so poor that he could not even afford a pair of shoes. He had suffered great illness. He had lost close family members. You name it, it had happened to Reb Zusha.

The *chassidim* traveled a long way to find Reb Zusha and confronted him with the same question. Why did bad things happen to good people? His response was simple:

"Why ask me? Nothing bad has ever happened to me."

He felt unqualified to answer the question, as it was purely theoretical for him. Life had been good to him and nothing bad had ever really happened to him. Painful, yes. Difficult, yes. But bad? No way.

He was not putting on a show for them; he meant every word he said. Everything he had been through had brought him closer to God. From his perspective, his life was filled with true goodness. Poverty had brought him closer to God. Illness had brought him closer to God. Losing those he loved had brought him closer to God. So where was the bad? He certainly didn't perceive it. There was pain, but much of it had passed and that which had not yet passed would also pass. He had faced his challenges and achieved greatness through them.

Reb Zusha's response to his tests brought him closer to God. Some may have responded in the same way. Yet others would have chosen, albeit innocently, to distance themselves from their Creator. It is all up to us; it is our choice.

The Holocaust

This idea of the supremacy of personal choice is true even in the most extreme of circumstances. I have met many survivors of the Holocaust, all of whom were put through the most horrific experiences. There are those whose response was to turn away from God, but for some, it brought them even closer. It is a common myth to believe that the Holocaust pushed all those who experienced it away from God. Those who did distance themselves from God are perhaps more vociferous, but there are many others who responded very differently.

Before I go further, let me state that it is not for us, who did not go through such horrors, to judge those who did. We did not experience their pain and terror and are in no position to question why they did what they did. But one thing is clear. While the experience itself was not in their hands, their response to it was. Some chose to turn away from God; some chose to find solace and renewed faith in God. For those who turned away from God, it was their free choice that caused them to do so, not the Holocaust. To be sure, the Holocaust was a catalyst. But for many, also, the Holocaust was a catalyst for coming closer to their Creator. That was their choice also. The fact that people can come through the Holocaust with such difference responses shows clearly that it was not the circumstances that caused the response, rather it was their own choices. If it was purely the event, then everyone's response should have been the same.

None of us can possibly know how we would have responded in those most horrific of circumstances and, as I have already said, it is not for us to pass judgment. But one thing is for sure — whatever might be denied us in this world, the ability to choose to grow from our experiences or to become resentful can never be taken away from us. We are all complete masters of our own spiritual destiny.

One of my most significant insights into this aspect of the Holocaust came in Krakow's old Jewish cemetery. I had brought a group of young Jews to Poland to gain a deeper understanding of the Holocaust, and we were accompanied by a survivor. As Holocaust experiences go, his had been pretty "bad." He was a member of the Sonderkommando in Birkenau. For eleven months, in 1944, he had worked in Crematoria II, taking the still warm bodies of Hungarian Jewry from the gas chambers and putting them in the ovens. He was a direct eyewitness to the murder of hundreds of thousands of Jews. Day after day, for eleven months, he saw the door of a gas chamber close on two thousand living, breathing human beings and saw it open, fifteen minutes later, to a twisted mass of lifeless flesh.

Our group asked him how he felt about God and he said that his belief in God had died in Birkenau. There could be no God after what he had seen.

On our way back from Auschwitz with him, we were visiting the old Jewish cemetery in Krakow and we bumped into another survivor who happened to be an Orthodox Jew. He had been in the Lodz Ghetto and eight different camps, including Auschwitz. He had now brought his two sons from Australia to see where he had grown up. Members of our group were bold enough to ask the question that was on all of our minds — mine included. How could he be an Orthodox Jew after all he had gone through?

We were shocked by the ferocity of the answer he shot back. How could someone not believe in God after the Holocaust? Anyone who survived had to have experienced miracles. In fact, the Holocaust itself was completely supernatural — that the Germans should wish to utterly eliminate a sector of the population that posed no threat to them whatsoever. It made no sense at all without putting God in the picture, was his response.

Not only that, he said, but he would challenge any survivor who did not believe in God on these issues. He said that a survivor might be angry at God. He might want nothing to do with God. He might even hate God. But he could not possibly believe that there was no God.

We mentioned what the survivor who was with our group had said to us and he asked to meet him. Nervously, I introduced them. I don't remember exactly what words passed between them, or how they were said. I just remember that it was passionate and powerful, and for twenty minutes the group stood transfixed listening to the debate. By the end of it all, the survivor who was with us admitted that he did believe in God, but after what he had been through, he did not want to deal with Him anymore. They cried, they embraced, and the other survivor said that he understood.

The second survivor told me he could argue the same point with any other survivor. That's a bold statement, but one thing is for sure, the Holocaust, as with all tragedy, has aspects that can move one away from God; but it equally has aspects that can move one closer. What actually happens is entirely within our human hands.

Suffering

At this point, I want to draw an important distinction based on what I have been talking about — the difference between pain and suffering. I have been using the words loosely until now, but they are in actuality subtly, yet very significantly, different.

We all go through pain in this world. It comes at us from the outside. Suffering, however, is self-inflicted. It depends entirely on how we respond to our pain. If we see pain as something real, something tangible and important, then we will suffer. If we see beyond the pain to a deeper truth, then we may still go through the pain, but we do not have to suffer.

Day after day, month after month, year after year, I watched Elana in pain — if not physical, then emotional. She desperately wanted to see her children grow up; she wanted to dance at their weddings, but knew in her heart of hearts that she never would. She went through immense anguish.

Never once, however, did I see her suffer. Not a single moment. What she wanted to do with her time was in the foreground of her consciousness. Pain, whilst still there, took a back seat. It didn't matter to her as much.

We can see the same thing in less extreme cases. When a woman gives birth, she goes through tremendous pain, but does she suffer? Bringing up children can be incredibly difficult. Some may call it painful. But is it ever 'suffering'? Running a marathon is overwhelmingly painful for the last few miles (and if you are as unfit as I am, then for all the miles previous to that also!), but people do it willingly because it is not suffering.

I think the distinction between pain and suffering is as follows:

When pain matters to us more than anything else, we suffer. When it does not, we do not. The more we have in life that matters to us over and above the pain, the more that pain recedes into the background. When nothing matters more than the pain we are going through, it comes into intense focus and overwhelms us. That overwhelmingness, we refer to as suffering.

The simple ability to put pain into a meaningful context enables us to see beyond it. Elana used to quote Nietzche saying, "A man can deal with any 'what', as long as he has a good enough 'why'."

A child, for example, cuts his finger and screams the house down. An adult cuts his finger and gets on with life. Children live in the moment, so there is only pain — no context. An adult realizes that the pain will pass and life will be good again in spite of it. He doesn't suffer. And, by the way, why is it that when you hug and kiss a child the pain seems to go away in a moment? It's not the pain that goes, it's the suffering. You have shown the child something that matters more — a parent's love. The pain may still be there physically – but the child no longer suffers.

As adults, we do best when we see beyond our own pain to something more. Sometimes it is obvious to us, as in the case of a marathon or a woman in labor. Sometimes it is a little harder. But whenever we can find something that matters to us more – even in the midst of our pain, the suffering will be over.

Conclusion

As I said at the beginning, bad things do not happen to anyone.

Pain certainly happens. And it doesn't distinguish between good and bad people. (I only mean 'good' and 'bad' people in terms of perception. In reality, who is any one of us to judge who is good and who is bad? But when people ask the question — "why do bad things happen to good people" — they are referring to people we perceive as good or bad. So I am using that definition as reference for this point, even though I do not agree with it.) Sometimes a lot of pain happens to people. Sometimes tragic and horrific pain happens to people — good people included. But whether pain leads to suffering or not is dependent entirely on choice. A healthy response to pain is not indicative of a good or bad person; it is just a sign of whether the person will grow closer to God or not as a result of this specific experience.

The point remains the same — circumstances are neutral. We and we alone, make the choice of whether they are to be good or bad.

Chapter 2
Why a World of Pain?

All that I have said so far still leaves us with a question. Yes, maybe pain does help us grow and develop. Maybe it is not a 'bad' thing after all. But that doesn't take away from the fact that it is still a painful thing. It might not be 'bad,' but whichever way you look at it, it is unpleasant. Why couldn't God have simply created a world without any pain at all?

The answer lies in understanding the nature of God.

When Moses stands at the burning bush, he asks God what he should tell the Jewish people. Who should he say is sending him to free them from Egypt? God's answer is very enigmatic: "I will be what I will be" (Exodus 3:14). He then tells Moses to tell the Jewish people, "'I will be' has sent you." My Microsoft grammar-checker doesn't like that one, but Moses seems quite satisfied with the answer. He somehow understands this phrase as a deep insight into the essence of God. Allow me to explain what I believe the Torah is telling us.

Everything in creation is defined by and influenced by external forces. An animal is firstly defined by its own particular DNA. Once created, it is now shaped by its environment — its mother, its experiences, its needs and lackings. A lion brought up in a zoo will be a very different lion than one allowed to roam free in the jungle — even if they have identical DNA.

Human beings also have this nature versus nurture business, but we have an added dimension — that of freewill. We are firstly influenced by the external forces in our makeup — the nature of our genes — both physical and spiritual. Once we come into the world, there is nurture and experience. But there is also freewill — the ability to choose and shape our own destiny. You will often hear of the "nurture/nature" debate — which of the two factors is more significant in human development. We Jews agree with neither side. What truly has the potential to shape us is our freewill, who we decide we want to be. God, however, is completely different from anything in this world. Whereas our world is one of form, He is completely formless.

He is the Infinite Spiritual Essence that is manifest in form through our world. He is "One" — completely unique, and incomparable to any aspect of His creation. There is no external force that can shape Him for He is the creator of all forces. There is no existence external to Him. There are no genes that dictated His form. He is defined by one thing and one thing alone — what He is. His essence defines Him. He is not subjected to the limitation of the whims of freewill — even His own. This is not a limitation of freewill; quite the opposite, it is freewill in its perfect form. He is what He is and "will be what He will be." His essence defines Him as perfect, so He cannot make a 'decision' to be imperfect. And that essence can never change.

He is not affected by his environment in any way because He is his environment. He is formless and all of form is only a manifestation of Him. Nothing can affect Him because nothing is separate from Him.

This is what God meant when He said, "'I will be' has sent you."

Moses understood that God wanted him to say this to the Jewish People. The God who was sending Moses was the formless, and hence detached, God; the God Who is above and beyond all the trivialities of mankind; the God who is Supreme, Infinite and Perfect. If the Jewish People would see God in this way, it would lift their sights from the pettiness of their own suffering The details would become irrelevant in the face of God's utter transcendence.

Now we can take a look at creation and see why adversity is an unavoidable element. God, the Infinite Being, created a universe as a natural consequence of His existence. It was a higher level of choice — based not on personal decision, but rather on absolute reality. Perfection means giving, and giving requires a recipient. So, in effect, God 'needs' a universe to which He can give.

However, there is only one thing that God can give and that is Himself. He is, after all, all that exists!

The goodness that He gives, therefore, is the experience of the infinite, of reality, of Him. And herein lies the paradox. God wants to create beings with whom He can have a relationship, but if they are to be takers, then they will be His complete opposite — He will be the absolute giver, His creations, the absolute takers. How then can a relationship exist? Relationships are built upon commonality. If we were to be complete takers, we would have nothing in common with God.

As a result, He had to create a mechanism in which the beings He created would be able to feel that they earned their intimacy with Him. They would struggle to be like Him and, in so doing, they would come close to Him. This is why God created the concept of freewill. The only way for God to be able to give in a meaningful way is for Him to create beings who can choose for themselves. They can choose whether or not to be Godly.

And for freewill to be at all meaningful, it must be real. There must be very real opportunities to move away from Godliness. If it is all a sham, then it serves no purpose. We need real decisions with real consequences.

So God, in His infinite wisdom, created two stages to our existence. First is a stage when we can use our freewill to 'earn' our relationship with Him. And second is a stage in which we can enjoy the closeness to God which we have earned. This is the reason for this world and the next.

But why would a being that God created choose to move away from Godliness? In a Godly world, why would it want anything else?

Because God created an illusion. The illusion that we know as our world. An illusion that looks so real, that seems so tangible, that is so three dimensional, that we are attracted to it like iron to a magnet. God, the Spiritual World, is all that is real. But God has created a world of thought through which we have human experiences. Our "thought world" is a distraction from the truth of the spiritual world. But it is so compelling at times that we find ourselves simply unable to see beyond it.

This is where we can exercise our freewill. We can follow the compulsion of an illusionary, but often times, attractive world, or see beyond that illusion to a deeper truth.

Pain is part of the illusion. And when it comes on strong and tangible it plays a significant role in putting us in a position of choice. Follow where it leads: To the world of our own very real looking personal thinking or choose to see past it to a more peaceful and truthful spiritual experience.

The purpose of this world is choice — to give us the incredible opportunity to be independent beings, to live our own lives, to be ourselves. It's what makes the whole thing worthwhile; and pain, or rather the very real illusion of pain, is a big part of it.

Pain, an illusion, you say? It seems very real to me!

Well, yes actually…

Did you ever have a filling done? The dentist takes out a very nasty looking drill which whizzes around at millions of miles an hour and he digs a very large hole into your very sensitive tooth. So where did all the pain go? Well, there's a little secret called anesthetic.

I recall having an operation on my hand when I broke a bone many years ago and needed pins to keep it in place. They gave me a local anesthetic and then cut a massive slice into my hand (without me watching of course) then placed the necessary pins. I was wide awake and felt absolutely nothing. Why? Because we are blessed to live in a generation in which we have anesthetics. But how do these anesthetics work? Well here's what they don't do. They don't make your hand all numb so that it feels nothing. What they do is they simply block the nerves that send messages of pain to the brain and without a message of pain, the brain cannot feel pain. In other words, said simply, we feel pain in our brain, not in our hand. Even though it seems for all the world to us that it's happening in our hand. But that can't be because when a person has a local anesthetic, the hand goes through exactly the same experience but there is zero pain.

In other words again, pain is created by thought. In fact, pain is a thought itself.

Remember those times when you have cut yourself but don't notice because you are too busy? You walk around with a bleeding finger and feel no pain. You finish what you are doing and look down. Lo and behold, you see blood — and almost immediately feel pain. If we are not conscious, for one reason or another, of the thought of pain, then pain does not exist.

Physical pain is an illusion, a 3D technicolor illusion, but an illusion nevertheless. When we don't notice the illusion, it doesn't exist in our experience.

But as I have said, there are times when the illusion is so compelling, that we get lost in how real it all seems and forget that there is anything beyond it.

Again, at times like this we are at the cutting edge of our own free choice.

Pain is part of the illusion and adversity is part of the illusion also — often a part that seems very, very real.

So this world is a series of perceived tests over which to triumph, so that we can gradually become more Godly human beings.

With this in mind, it also makes sense that the closer one gets to God, the greater the trials must be. If a person has overcome an easy test, thus actualizing a certain amount of potential, then the next stage must be more difficult. Those who face increasingly challenging circumstances should be the people getting things right — because they are the ones who will benefit most.

The greatest reward a person could want for overcoming a difficult challenge is an even harder challenge — a greater opportunity to choose to see beyond the illusion, to assert independence and hence to connect ever more deeply to God. I mentioned earlier that Abraham was tested with ten tests "to show how much he was beloved before God." Each of these tests was more challenging than the one before, until he reached the pinnacle of human greatness, ready to transcend this world into the more beautiful and more perfect world that awaited him.

We Jews do not ask for challenges. Who is arrogant enough to believe he will overcome them? We are all human after all. Yet, when they come, we relish our challenges, for they are the true opportunities of life.

As such, if we define bad as something challenging, then contrary to what we might initially have expected, 'bad' will probably happen to good people more often than to anyone else.

Corrective Pain

C hallenging us to greatness is the primary purpose of pain, but there is also a secondary purpose.

As I said earlier, in order for freewill not to be a sham, the option to choose to move away from God must be a real one. We must be able to drift away and then away again and then still further.

Let's say one of God's created beings does this. Now God has three choices, none of which are all that appealing:

1. God can take away the person's freewill and bring him back by force — hence rendering His existence in this world utterly meaningless (as freewill is the purpose of the world). He would do this person a greater service by simply removing him from the world.

2. God can choose to do nothing and allow the person to continue His course of action. This would make the person's existence worse than meaningless. Not only would he not be accomplishing God's purpose for him being created, but he would actually be moving farther and farther away from it.

3. God can create a world of consequences to mistaken paths; He can make it that ultimately, going down a wrong path brings disappointment and dissatisfaction.

These three choices are the same ones parents have with their children. Take, for example, a child who is becoming involved with drugs. His parents have a number of choices:

1. They can lock him in his room forever — thus solving the problem, but rendering his life meaningless. He may be unable to take anymore drugs, but he cannot do anything else in life either.

2. They can take no action and allow him to continue doing drugs — taking the risk that he may ultimately quite literally destroy himself. This would probably be the most callous of all decisions a parent can make.

3. They can create natural consequences to his actions, so that there is pain commensurate to his mistakes — not so much pain that it takes away his free choice, but enough to help him realize that

perhaps this is not how he wants to live. They could threaten to cut off money or other benefits he has been enjoying — perhaps even throw him out of the house.

In drug counselling, we are told that the only time at which many addicts start on the process of rehabilitation is when they have reached rock bottom; when they are penniless, on the streets, with no friends and no one to help them. At that point, they often realize that drugs are destroying their life and they become open to listening to something new. Only the pain of their situation is strong enough to shake them out of the apathy that their own ego has innocently trapped them in.

Difficult as it might be for parents, creating painful consequences is sometimes the only way to intervene with children in distress.

It is also something God has programmed in to our world to help us keep oriented in a direction of Godliness and spiritual development.

When we make mistakes, there are consequences so that we may wake up to the fact that this is not how we want to be living. We might wake up, but then again, we might not. Freewill remains a constant. There is a message, but it is only effective if we respond in the correct way. The consequences are not strong enough to compel us to change; they are merely there to gently coax us in the right direction. The choice, as always, is our own.

Pain and hardship are often (though not always) God's means of waking us up to mistakes we are making. This is not punishment. It is a wake-up call for us to rediscover our purpose in life.

The Rabbis tell us that when a person sees troubles coming upon him, he should examine his deeds *(Berachos 5a)*. Pain, in addition to being a crucial cog in the mechanism for freewill, is also used to convey a message. It is not a punishment. It is there to tell us that we are doing something wrong — to show us that we need to adjust our mode of action.

And pain is not really a direct response to our actions. Judaism looks at it more as a cause and effect system.

Just as there is physical cause and effect, so too there is spiritual cause and effect. We don't say that if you jump off a building, God will punish you by pulverizing your body. We say that God created a world such that if you jump off a building, your body will be pulverized as a direct consequence of hitting the hard ground at great velocity. Similarly, we say that if you jump off a spiritual building, there will be consequences — not punishments — consequences.

Pain, therefore, serves two purposes.

First, it creates challenges through which we can choose to come closer to God. This is what the *Mishnah (Ethics of the Fathers 5:4)* says, "God tested Abraham with ten tests, to show how great was His love for Abraham."

And second, it is used as a mechanism for waking us up to our mistakes.

There is a third purpose for pain found in rabbinic writings, which is the concept of *kapparah*, atonement. I don't want to go deeply into this topic, but in simple terms it is a more sophisticated extension of the second aspect of pain. God does not bring pain to cleanse us of our transgressions. *Kapparah* enables a person who has already changed his direction in the necessary way, to find the deepest levels of oneness with that change.

An example might be that of a person who overindulges in food. He then comes to a realization that this is wrong and as a result goes through a process of self-correction. However, it's all a little cerebral, and staying up all night with a stomach-ache will make his understanding of his own stupidity much more deeply felt. God might do this for him in order that he can internalize the lesson more deeply and fully.

A wealthy man who turned his back on poor people but has now realized his mistake and become very generous might still not have had a deep enough realisation for the change to be complete until he has been lost in a desert for a week with little food or drink and with no one to reach out to him.

You might assume from this that those making the most mistakes in life should go through the most pain.

But there is another factor to take into account.

Let's say you have two children. One does well in school. He is a loving, caring, diligent child. He has a good crowd of friends and spends his spare time visiting his grandparents or furthering his quest for wisdom. He excels at all that he does and is loved by all.

Your other child, however, is the type who just can't seem to get his life in order. He's a failure in school. He's in with the wrong crowd. He's rude and abusive to his parents and others around him and never does anything for anyone other than himself.

One day, you hear that your two children have been out shoplifting together. You cannot believe it, but the facts are undeniable. With which one would you be more disappointed?

It's obvious that you would be more disappointed with the 'good' child, with the child who usually gets things right. From the child who is struggling, you'd expect such a thing. But from the child who is doing so well — to steal?! He has set his standards so high that your expectations are also high, and therefore, your anger and frustration are much greater.

The same is true of God and His children. The Sages tell us that God judges the righteous "to a hair's breadth" (*Yevamos* 121a). Those who come close to Him are held much more accountable for their actions than those who are distant. God expects more from them because they expect more from themselves.

Why would God try to teach someone a lesson if they have no interest in learning it? As we have mentioned before, "God leads a person in the way he wants to go."

As I said earlier, the Sages make a remarkable statement: "A person who has had nothing painful happen to him in forty days has 'acquired his world.'"

How is it possible for a human being to go for forty days without either a challenge or a wake-up call? Why has God put him or her in this world if not to grow? It cannot be that this person is completely righteous, for in such a case, while he would perhaps need no wake-up calls, his challenges would nevertheless increase because God constantly pushes the righteous to grow more, achieve more, develop more — to help lift them to greater levels of Godliness.

The only possible scenario for an effortless forty-day period is as follows: A person becomes so distant from God that challenges will only push him further away and wake-up calls will achieve nothing. Such a person will be unable to experience God in a future existence. But for the few good choices he must have made during his lifetime, God is able to give him some level of goodness in this world. It's not considered a punishment to grant him goodness in this world, as opposed to in the next. As one so completely tied to this world, it's a consequence. It's the only place in which he will be able to appreciate any goodness that is bestowed. Therefore, such a person will receive a life of goodness, with no challenges and no setbacks for the period of time his amount of goodness has earned him. He will be given his 'next world' in this one — hence the phrase "acquired his world." Forty days without any trouble whatsoever is a very clear sign that a person is in such a situation.

In Judaism we view "problems", far from being something bad, they are a sign of spiritual vigour and vibrancy!

The more a person moves forward, the more he or she will be faced with challenge and difficulty.

This may not sound like much of an incentive to grow spiritually, but that is only if you look at pain as a 'bad' thing. Pain, in actual fact, is neutral; a wonderful means through which to find the deepest of spiritual experiences.

The China Teacup

I once read a lovely story. I'll quote it exactly as I heard it.

A couple once took an anniversary trip to England and were shopping in a shop of beautiful things.

They both liked antiques and pottery, and especially teacups. Spotting an exceptional cup, the woman said, "May we see that? It's so beautiful…"

As the lady handed the teacup to them, suddenly it began to speak, "You don't understand. I have not always been a teacup. There was a time when I was just a lump of red clay.

My master took me and rolled me and pounded and me, over and over, and I yelled out, 'Don't do that. I don't like it! Leave me alone!' But he only smiled, and said, 'Not yet…'

Then, WHAM! I was placed on a spinning wheel and spun around and around.

'Stop it! I'm getting dizzy! I'm going to be sick!' I screamed.

But the master only nodded and said quietly, 'Not yet.'

He spun me and poked and prodded and bent me out of shape to suit himself and then…then he put me in an oven. I had never felt such heat. I yelled and knocked and pounded at the door. 'Help! Get me out of here!'

I could see him through the glass door and I could read his lips as he shook his head from side to side, 'Not yet.'

When I thought I couldn't bear it another minute, he opened the door, carefully took me out, and put me on a shelf, where I began to cool. Oh, that felt so good! 'This is much better,' I thought. But, after I cooled off, he picked me up and brushed me and painted me all over. The fumes were horrible. I thought I would gag. 'Oh, please! Stop it, stop it!' I cried. He only shook his head and said. 'Not yet.'

Then, suddenly, he put me back in the oven. Only it was not like the first one. This oven was twice as hot, and I just knew I would suffocate. I begged. I pleaded. I screamed. I cried. I was convinced I would never make it. I was ready to give up.

Just then the door opened and he took me out and again placed me on the shelf, where I cooled off and waited, wondering, 'What's coming next?'

Then he handed me a mirror and said, 'Look at yourself.' And I did. 'That's not me!' I said. 'That couldn't be me. It's beautiful…I'm beautiful!'

And then he spoke: 'I know it hurt to be rolled and pounded and patted, but had I left you alone, you would have dried up. I know it made you dizzy to spin around on the wheel, but if I had stopped, you would have crumbled. I know it was hot and you suffered terribly in the oven, but if I hadn't put you there, you would have cracked. I know the fumes were bad when I painted you, but if I hadn't done that, you never would have hardened. You never would have had any color in your life. And if I hadn't put you in that second oven, you wouldn't have survived for long, because your hardness would not have held.

Now you are a finished product. Now you are what I had in mind when I first began with you."

God is the potter, and we are His clay. He will mold us and make us, and expose us to just enough pressures of just the right kinds that we may become a flawless piece of work to fulfill His good, pleasing, and perfect will.

So when life seems hard, and you are being pounded and pushed almost beyond endurance; when your world seems to be spinning out of control; when you feel you're in a fiery furnace of trials; when life seems to "stink," of awful fumes, try this...

Brew a cup of your favorite tea, in your prettiest tea cup. Then sit down and think of this story and...have a little talk with the Potter.

(Author unknown)

Chapter 3
Death

Okay, you might say, that is pain and maybe all pain is an opportunity to grow closer to God. But what about death? Isn't death the termination of that opportunity? What about someone who dies young? How can that possibly be good?

Judaism assures us that this life is not the be all and end all. In fact, this life is only a 'corridor' to the next world — which is the main realm of human existence. While this world is for seventy or eighty years, the next world is for eternity. This world is very much a side show to the main event.

Just as if life is about avoiding pain, there is no answer for why painful things happen, so too, if this world is the sum total of human existence, there is no answer for how people can die young.

Following on from what I said in my introduction, in any case, both questions are meaningless outside of the context of God. For the atheist, the answer as to why bad things happen and people die young is simple, though perhaps uncomfortable. We live in a random world. And people die young because this random world does not distinguish between young and old. A falling tree or a cancer cell cannot and will not distinguish between someone who is 'good' and someone who is 'bad,' someone who has lived a full life and someone who has not. Only when we talk about God do these questions have any relevance. And if we are to ask these questions according to the axioms of Monotheism, we must accept an answer in the same vein. And the concept of a next world is as axiomatic to Monotheism as natural selection is to Evolution.

I could, at this point, give a very simple, though deeply unsatisfying answer to our question of people dying young. I could merely say that death is not a bad thing because the soul goes to a better world. It is happier, more fulfilled, and has a deeper connection with God. In fact, pushing the idea to its extreme, one could say that death is just about the best thing that could happen to a person!

This is obviously not a satisfactory answer, because if death is so wonderful and should happen to everyone as soon as possible, why did God create us in this world in the first place? Why not put us all into the next world straight away?

In simple terms, this world is also good and leaving it 'early' cannot be justified by a next world alone. I, for one, require a more sophisticated answer than this.

Dying Young

"And God saw that it was very good..." (Genesis 1:31). The *Midrash (Bereishis Rabbah* 9:12) asks what was created on the sixth day of creation that was "very good" versus the other five days which were only "good"? "Very good," it explains, refers to the angel of death! Death, in Judaism, is not only not very bad — it is actually very good. It is a very necessary element of this realm of existence, without which we would struggle to accomplish anything. And it's not good just because you go to a better world. It's a very good thing in and of itself.

Elana always used to say that if you lived forever, why would you bother to get up in the morning? You wouldn't need to accomplish anything today; you could always do it tomorrow. And if you didn't do it tomorrow, there would always be the next day. And if not the next day, you could do it in a thousand years or so. Why start your diet today when you can start it in ten thousand years? If life is forever, there's plenty of time for everything. Who needs to capture the moment — when there are an infinite amount of moments to be captured?

The fact that there is quite literally a "deadline" to life means that we have to get on with it. And the fact that the deadline is uncertain means that we cannot rely on tomorrow for accomplishment, because there may not be a tomorrow. Today is all that we have. The Rabbis tell us, "Repent one day before you die" *(Ethics of the Fathers 2:15).*

How do you know which day is the one before you die? You don't, so do it today and every day. One of these days you will get it right!

Not knowing when we'll die creates, if we allow it to, a very real and healthy sense of urgency to get on with life.

In fact, knowing when death is really imminent is something of a luxury. It focuses a person's attention in a way that nothing else can. I still vividly remember our oncologist calling me in to her office, six weeks before Elana died. The words she said, "Time is very short," are still etched in my memory. For the last six weeks of her life, when Elana knew that time was very, very short, she made use of every moment. And I made use of every moment with her. Our relationship in general was a very good one, but if we could have lived during our whole marriage the way we lived for those last six weeks, it would have been absolutely unbelievable. Unfortunately, the feeling that we have all the time in the world generates a certain sense of complacency. For six weeks, we were in no way complacent about our relationship. We didn't allow petty things to get in the way of our love for each other. And I look back on that time as being the time in my life when I was most alive. Elana felt the same way. Every second is always precious. But during those weeks, every second was not just precious but cherished.

So often, I wish that I could return to that deep and intimate experience of time being short. Reality has not changed, but illusion has taken over again. Time is as short for me now as it was for us then. If only I could feel it in the way I did during those six weeks, I know I would live my life very differently.

So the Rabbis are telling us that death is a wonderful reality that God has created in order to focus us on the goodness that we have right now. And they are, as always, careful in their language. They do not say that "death" is very good. They say that the "angel of death" is very good. The fact that we know there is an "angel of death" who will call upon us one day without necessarily ringing the bell first has the potential to wake us up to the goodness of life. It is not so much death that is good, but our awareness of death's certainty that is good. And it is not just "good," it is "very good."

Death, ironically, makes us wake up and live. And the fact that people die at various ages — some even very young — should make us realize that we can take nothing for granted. If everyone lived until ninety, we would not use our time effectively at twenty or thirty or forty. We need death and we need the fact that people die young to remind us that the end can come at any moment. To remind us to live today in a way that we do not take tomorrow for granted.

But this is still not enough of an answer.

It might explain why some people die young, but still leaves us with a burning question as to why God chooses some and not others. And why does it so often seem that "Only the good die young" (to quote a popular song as I was growing up)?

It's All Relative

We have already dealt with two mistaken premises: First, that pain is bad and second, that death is bad. The former misleads us to believe that bad things do actually 'happen' to good people. The latter misleads us to believe that when people die, we must question why God would do this to them.

To answer the final question of why specific people die at a young age, I need to bring in a third mistaken premise, which is that God owes us something; that there is a certain amount that is due a human being in this world and anything less is unfair.

Let's say that I give you $10,000. It is a free gift out of the goodness of my heart. I don't know you. You have done nothing to earn it.

What would you say to me? Or rather, what *should* you say to me? "Thank you very much," I would hope.

Okay, there you are feeling really good. I just gave you $10,000 as a present. And now I go over to your best friend and hand him $50,000. Again, I give it as a free gift — no strings attached. I don't know your friend any better than I know you and he has done as little as you to merit my kindness.

Now how do you feel about your $10,000? Not quite the same? Why did I only give you $10,000 when I gave your friend $50,000? Why is he more deserving than you are? All of a sudden, my $10,000 does not seem like the wonderful and generous gift that it was a few minutes ago.

This is plain and simple human nature. We don't judge what we have in absolute terms. We compare it to what others have. $10,000 is great — until my friend gets $50,000. Now my $10,000 looks like nothing, because of what I could (and in my mind, should) have been granted. And if he had been given the $50,000, why not me? As my friend whizzes by my brand new Mini in his brand new Porsche, my $10,000 seems almost like a curse.

It's crazy, but we all compare in this way. One of the great challenges of this world is to appreciate and enjoy what we ourselves have — even though there are others who have more.

This mistake of comparing to others is so pervasive that we often don't even notice just where and how much it is affecting us. We might not realize, but it is the main issue that bothers us when talking about why people die young.

What is "young"?

"Young" is a completely relative term that should have no real meaning when looking at the wonderful gift of life that we have been given.

The Bible says that people used to live hundreds of years. Let's try to imagine a society in which that were the case — say that people usually died in their nine hundreds. Now, what would we say about a righteous man who died at one hundred years old? We would say it was terrible, a tragedy. He was cut down in his prime. We would ask ourselves the burning question — why do bad things happen to good people? And Billy Joel would write a song saying, "Only the good die young."

Let's take a look at the other side of the coin. In the Middle Ages, people used to live until thirty-five. So what would we say about someone who, like Elana, died at thirty? She lived to a ripe old age. She was blessed with a long and fruitful life.

The simple truth is that God owes us nothing — absolutely nothing. All He gives us is a free and wonderful gift. If we view the world with this in mind, it takes on a very different hue.

Life until now has been a gift. And every extra moment of life is another added gift. Be it one thousand years of extra moments or one hundred years of extra moments or thirty years or ten or five years, or five months or five weeks or even five days...each and every moment remains a gift. Every moment is precious. Every moment is special. Every moment is something to be thankful for, instead of complaining about the moments that we or others were not granted.

Why God might choose to give one person a larger gift than someone else is really not for us to ask. Even the smaller gift is still an incredible one — and is not in any way diminished by the fact that others get larger ones. God has every right to give one person a great deal and another person even more. It's not unfair. As the one giving, it's His prerogative to give as He sees fit. And for us to complain is an incredible lack of appreciation for the magnitude of what has been given to us in the first place. My previous analogy of $50,000 and $10,000 is completely understated. It is more like someone complaining that he was only given $10 billion, while his friend was given $50 billion.

Look at how ridiculous it is. We are observing an individual created by God. As a created being, he 'deserves' nothing. But then, look! He is given $10 billion worth of free gifts — he is given life, freewill, emotions, a mind, family, friends, passion, arms and legs, vision, hearing, energy, talents...and the list goes on. And he is given all of these gifts for thirty-five whole years. Incredible! Do we respond by feeling that God is a wonderful giver? No, we complain that he got a raw deal. Only $10 billion instead of $50 billion? Really and truly, we are crazy!

This is the first point in my answer: surely it is inappropriate to question the giver of a gift as to whether it is large enough, because a gift is a good and blessed thing, no matter how small.

But there is another aspect, as well.

It may, in fact, be the case that all our gifts are exactly equal. Perhaps one person (Elana, for example) received a loftier soul and hence needed to spend less time in this world. Perhaps another person finished his or her task in this world and was ready to move on to a better place — which the next world surely is. Perhaps another person was given more material wealth, more intelligence, more love, but received less time. And yet another who did not receive these gifts was given more time instead. Who are we simple humans to know God's calculations?

Our children's favorite phrase seems to be, "It's not fair." I'm sure every parent hears that line regularly. Why did one get more than the other? Or even if they got the same, their friends got things that they didn't get. And even if they got more than their friends, still they did not get as much as they would have liked and it's all just so unfair. It's like a chorus in my house. I would estimate I hear it about twenty times a day. One of my many standard answers is as appropriate for this book as it is for my children. I will ask my sons, "If I were to buy your sisters a doll, would you want me to be perfectly fair and buy you one also?" And I ask my daughters, "If I bought your brothers a football, would you want one, as well?" Do they all want to wear nappies because the baby does? Of course not. Fair does not mean everyone getting exactly the same thing — it means each getting according to his or her particular needs. And this varies not just for male and female, young and old, but for every single individual. Even were I to feel (which I don't) that absolute equality was something important for my children, they would nevertheless end up with very different things.

The same concept of fairness is true for God. God metes out His blessings in perfectly equal measure to everyone. Not everyone gets the same, but everyone gets an equal amount of God's goodness. To judge fairness on one issue alone — that of length of life — is absurd.

Whether we are given one thousand minutes, days, weeks, months, or even years, it's fair. It's not the same, but it's fair and equal. Until we have all the facts in front of us, we will not be able to see it, but since God is the infinite being, we can trust He knows what He's doing and knows what is the ultimate fair deal.

As a final point on this topic, the *Kabbalists* talk about the concept of *gilgul neshamos* — Reincarnation. This is the belief that for various reasons, souls might return to this world in new bodies. One of those reasons might be that they have accomplished a great deal in their past life, but still have more to do. They have not quite completed the task of 'fixing' their soul. A short period of time in a new life would enable them to do so.

The Jewish concept is that the soul really does not want to be in this world in the first place. It would much rather be in the spiritual world that some call Heaven. It has a task to accomplish down here and it would rather be here for as short a time as possible. Maybe it only needs twenty years, or ten or five or maybe it only needs a few days or minutes in this world. If a person lived a short life, it might mean that they accomplished their mission and then moved on to a better world. It's only we who are left behind who feel the loss — not the one who died.

This is also one way of understanding a child who is born with Down's syndrome or any other similar condition. Their soul is one that has accomplished much and therefore needs fewer faculties to do what it now has to do. I heard it said that the *Chazon Ish* — possibly the greatest rabbi of the previous generation — used to stand up in respect if such a person walked into the room. He would say that they have a lofty soul and he wanted to show them due honor.

In summary of this section, pain is not bad. It is painful. Death is not bad. As a future certainty, it wakes us up to life. And when it happens, it takes us to a higher plane of existence. This world is one of frustration, challenge, difficulty, loss — but all of that leads us to the ultimate goal in this world, the attainment of Godliness, and it's well worth it.

Dreams and Nightmares

Psalm 126, *Shir HaMaalos*, states that when the present exile comes to an end, "We will be like dreamers." It will have been just a bad, albeit long, dream. Dreams are an amazing phenomenon — and a beautiful analogy for our life in this world. When you are in a dream, it all seems so real. You are not able to discern it as being illusion while you are experiencing it. As far as you are concerned, you are there and it is happening. Then you wake up. And suddenly, you realize that what you were experiencing was not real. You have no doubt that this is the case. You see it with complete clarity. As obviously real as it might have felt while you were in it, it is equally obviously unreal now that you are out of it.

This is especially true when the dream is a bad dream. It feels like you are really there. The nightmare is actually happening. You are being chased; you are falling; you are fighting; you are losing someone — whatever it might be. When you are within the nightmare, you do not understand it to be a dream. So you feel the terror, the horror, the pain. And then you wake up. The dream might linger momentarily, but very quickly, you realize that everything is okay. The nightmare was only a dream and the pain you felt was only an illusion. It's gone now, never to return. You relax immediately, and as quickly as it came, it is forgotten.

So too will it be, the Book of Psalms explains, with the exile of the Jewish people. The horror that the Jewish people has experienced during the last two thousand years — the torture, the inquisitions, the pogroms, the gas chambers, the suicide bombers...is a nightmare of the most massive proportions. But, the Rabbis explain, it is merely a nightmare. When the exile is over and the Jewish people are able to come close to God once again, when the good times finally arrive and the world returns to its state of perfection, the Jewish people, as a nation, will look back and feel it was all just a nightmare. When the world 'wakes up,' the dream will have vanished and the pain will be over — the purpose of it all will have been realized. Yes, it was painful at the time, but once it's over, the pain will be gone and forgotten.

This idea of the transience of pain is true not just on a national level, but also a personal level. The point is this: pain is only painful for as long as it exists. It never lingers. Any pain that remains with me with regards to losing Elana, for example, still remains with me not because the pain is lingering, but because Elana is still gone. Were she to miraculously return, the pain that I feel would dissipate immediately. In the same way, if you break a leg and then it heals, you feel no more pain. The fact that you felt pain when it was broken will not remain with you once it is better.

This is a part of the nature of pain — it is temporary. It is not self-sustaining. It will only last as long as the circumstance that causes it lasts. After that it is as nonexistent as a nightmare. There is no difference between real pain and a nightmare. When you feel the pain, it seems real — as though it will never end. The same is true with a nightmare. Afterwards, however, both are gone in their entirety — as though they never existed.

It's true that a person can replay the nightmare in his head and re-experience it, remind himself of it, put himself back into it mentally and feel the horror once again. And this is true of pain also.

People can torture themselves with something that is over and done with. They can cling to it and not let it go. But this ongoing pain is innocently self-inflicted. It is not the natural way of the world. For one reason or another, a person can choose to allow the pain to linger, can choose to be the conduit that sustains the pain through his own thinking of it. This is, once again, human choice, and God will always allow us our freewill. He leads us in the way that we want to go. Letting go happens when we realize it exists only in our thoughts. But if we ourselves, albeit innocently, choose to hold on to pain of our own thinking then we have no right to blame God that it still hurts.

We have all seen in our own lives the most painful of circumstances passing, and the pain disappearing as though it never existed. Think back to difficult and painful experiences you have had and see if remembering the pain bothers you at all. It is just a memory, perhaps a horrible memory, but it is not real. You can choose to let go of it.

The Talmud *(Niddah 31b)* gives us a clear example of how remembered pain does not have to affect us. It says that every woman who gives birth vows at some point during her labor that she will never do it again. The process is so painful that she cannot imagine repeating it. And yet, when the pain is gone, and all that remains is a beautiful new soul to love. Women go through labor, over and over again, in order to have more children. I have never heard of a woman who really wants more children stopping after one child due to the pain of labor. Once the pain is gone, she is ready to try again.

Much more often than not, every pain we experience will pass in this world. But even if it does not, it will certainly pass in the next. The pains and difficulties of this world will fade as fast as a nightmare does — no matter how real and intense they are at the time. We are talking moments, perhaps minutes or days or months and perhaps even years of living with pain — versus an eternity with that pain gone. In the context of eternity, even a lifetime of pain will be forgotten very quickly.

And then, as *Shir HaMaalos* continues, "Then, our mouths will be filled with laughter and our tongues with songs of praise." The pain that the Jewish people felt for millennia will disappear so quickly that we will spontaneously laugh in relief and joy. So, too, on a personal level. When the pain goes, we can laugh and break into song.

It seemed so real at the time, but now that it's gone, it's as if it never existed.

And that is the bottom line with pain. As real as it may seem when you are going through it, once it's gone, it's as though it never was. It's temporary. It passes. No pain lasts forever. If it does not pass in this world, it will certainly pass in the next.

Okay, you might say. Pain is not bad, it is merely painful. And pain is only real while it exists. But still, it's a very unpleasant experience. Why did a loving God create the concept of pain in the first place and why is it so prevalent in His world — so much a part and parcel of everyday life?

Chapter 4
Dealing with Pain

P ain is part and parcel of the human experience. There is no one who does not experience real and serious pain during their lifetime. And that pain will be physical, emotional, and spiritual. Like it or not, and not liking it is quite a natural response, it is a reality of our existence.

It is not fair or true to say that some people are forced to go through more pain than others. Pain is all relative to the person experiencing it. My wife, Chana, is able to have dental work done without anesthetic. I, on the other hand, cannot have a blood test without fainting. Pain is experienced differently by everyone and we cannot compare one person's pain to another's.

Pain is a given. And, as I have mentioned earlier, it is a wonderful given, for it enables us to connect to the infinite in a way that might otherwise be impossible. It's part of God's plan for a perfect world.

Unfortunately, especially in our generation, pain can often be looked upon as an enemy, something to be avoided, not embraced. Such an attitude is a sure-fire, though innocent, road to mediocrity. "No pain, no gain." Avoid challenges and meaningful accomplishment becomes nigh on impossible. Of course, we don't go looking for challenge, but avoiding it at all costs will only result in a society that misses out on much of the joy of life; a society that substitutes lasting pleasures for short-term excitement. A society like the one we live in today.

I often ask people what is the opposite of pain. Nine out of ten will immediately respond that it is pleasure. But when I press them to think more deeply, most appreciate that this is not the case. Think about it yourself before you continue. Is pleasure really the opposite of pain?

"Opposite," means diametrically opposed. They cannot exist together. You cannot have total dark and total light at the same time. Something cannot be alive and also dead. They are opposites and cannot coexist in the same object at the same point in time.

So now think about pain and pleasure for a minute. Can you experience pleasure while you are experiencing pain? When I go running, I reach a point where my eyes are stinging from the sweat running into them, my legs are aching, my lungs are bursting — every part of my body is crying out for me to give up. And yet I carry on — and I love it! It's not masochism, it's such a pleasure to ignore pain — and see beyond it to something more. It's pain and pleasure coexisting. The marathon runner who crosses the finish line is in absolute agony — and at the same time absolute ecstasy.

Pain and pleasure are not opposites.

The opposite of pain is, in fact, no pain. A total feeling of comfort. Pain and comfort cannot coexist. The marathon runner might experience deep pleasure, but he is not comfortable. He is in pain. It is impossible to be in pain and at the same time be comfortable. You are only comfortable to the extent that you are not in pain and only in pain to the extent you are not comfortable.

Pleasure, on the other hand, is something very different. We can experience pleasure, not in spite of pain, but because of it. Had the marathon runner been given a drug to make running a marathon as easy as walking down the street, he would experience very little pleasure when crossing the finish line. Transcending pain makes so many of life's pleasures that much more meaningful.

People will put themselves through inordinate amounts of pain in order to experience pleasure. Rabbi Weinberg often gave a very simple example. Imagine you took twenty-two men and told them to play soccer for ninety minutes — only, without a ball. They are to run around, tackle each other, kick, head, do all the things that one does when the ball is there, only the ball's not there! After ten minutes, they would be exhausted and unable to continue. The pain alone would be too much, without the pleasure of the game alongside it.

But once you throw a ball onto the field, everything changes. The same twenty-two men will run around like lunatics, jump, dive, puff, and pant — and absolutely love it. The great effort of the game is precisely what makes it pleasurable.

To define pleasure as the opposite of pain is misleading. Because in doing so, we associate pleasure with comfort (the true opposite of pain). And this simple misdefinition has significant ramifications. If pain is the opposite of pleasure — and of course pleasure is what human beings generally strive for — then pain must be avoided at all costs. Comfort becomes the be-all and end-all, and the search for one's ultimate good becomes the search for the easiest and most comfortable existence. In doing this, we may provide ourselves with lifestyles that are basically pain free, but it is unlikely that they will be filled with deep and lasting pleasure.

For example, many people are wary of the pain, effort, and expense involved in raising a large family. Some opt to avoid having children altogether. Life may be easier, but the new pleasure that comes with each child and the amazing satisfaction that comes from a large family's loving devotion and interconnections are completely missed.

Instead of the challenge and struggle of marriage, some couples opt out by living together; they avoid the risks, but also miss out on the depth of relationship that only total commitment can engender. Married couples are forced to confront issues head on, rather than sidestepping any unpleasantness. And only by grappling with issues do relationships deepen to their fullest extent. Living together is certainly easier — but the effort of marriage has the potential to bring infinitely deeper pleasure.

Instead of investing in our relationship with our children, do we put them in front of the television for a lot of the time? We might avoid the pain of spending time with them, but miss out on the pleasure of sharing their youth.

The problem is that seeking pleasure in the avoidance of pain just doesn't work, because avoiding the more superficial pains actually causes the deepest pain of all. As beings made in the image of God, our deepest pain is distance from Him. All other pains are transient, but this one is lasting. And so, by avoiding the pain of the moment, we condemn ourselves to a pain that will remain with us for eternity. By avoiding the struggle towards Godliness, we ensure that our lot is one of spiritual emptiness. How many television programs and movies can we watch? How much can a person run from one superficial high to the next until the hollowness of such an existence finally catches up? And even if he does manage to run for seventy years, in the grave there will be nowhere to run.

The way to find what we are looking for is by embracing and overcoming life's challenges. Elana and I came across many attitudes associated with doing well whilst going through a challenging time. I wish to share some of them with you in the following chapters.

And let me finish this section with one metaphor from my wife, Chana. Imagine that you are climbing a mountain. For various reasons you need to get to the top. And it's a long and challenging climb. You can't turn back or give up; the summit is where you need to get to. You have two choices. You can groan and grumble and feel frustrated and annoyed all the way up. Or you can accept what you need to do and enjoy the view as you go. In both instances, you will get to the top. But one way is so much more enjoyable than the other. Why would we choose to grumble and groan our way through life, when there is always such a beautiful view to be enjoyed along the way?

Chapter 5
Hashgacha,
Divine Providence

Moshe is late for a meeting and is desperately looking for a parking space in downtown Manhattan. As he's driving around in circles, he starts to pray, "Please, God, open up a parking space for me and I will pray with more meaning, spend more time with my wife, and study more seriously."

No sooner does he finish the sentence than a parking space miraculously appears right in front of him.

Moshe looks towards Heaven and says, "Not to worry, God. I already found one for myself!"

The Sages tell us, "When a man sees troubles coming upon him, he should examine his deeds. If he can find nothing that warrants such pain, he should assume it is due to *bitul Torah* [literally neglect of Torah study, but I understand the concept of *bitul Torah* here to mean something broader; he may not be doing anything wrong, but by the same token, he may not be putting in the proper effort to accomplish all that he is able to accomplish in his life.] If he can still find nothing that warrants such pain, he should assume it is *yissurin shel ahavah* (literally, 'troubles of love.')" *(Berachos 5a).*

I have often heard it said that we cannot understand why God causes us pain — why He makes 'bad' things happen to us. He has His reasons and who are we to try to understand? He is guiding our lives in the way we need to be guided but it doesn't necessarily have anything to do with our decisions or our actions. We can only trust that He knows what He's doing to us and we need to get on with our lives.

But for an Orthodox Jew, the Talmud is clear and unequivocal. If troubles come upon a person, the very first assumption he must make is that he has been doing something wrong. The troubles come, not as a punishment, but as a wake-up call. If he sees that he has done nothing to warrant this level of pain (Rashi's explanation of the Talmud), then he must move on to the assumption that in some way he is not actively doing enough. Only if he concludes that he really is doing all that he could be doing do we come to the *yissurin shel ahavah*, which, without going into too much detail, involves someone who has never made a mistake in this life, and who receives pain — without a direct message as such — in order to help him grow and develop into a greater and more Godly person. I believe the first two options cover the vast majority of situations, however, and so I will focus my attention on them.

Were it to be the case that the Talmud believes we cannot know the reason that pain happens to us, it should have said something very different. It should have said, "When a person sees troubles coming upon him, he should trust in God and know that there is a good reason for it." The Talmud does not say this. It says that he should look into his deeds.

Even if you say that it means sometimes we can figure out the reason for our pain and sometimes we can't, the next part of the Talmud disproves this: "If he can find nothing that warrants such pain, he should assume it is due to *bitul Torah*."

If the Talmud meant that sometimes we just can't know, it should not instruct us to take a next step — it should merely say that if you cannot figure out the answer, it must be one of those cases in which you don't know. But the Talmud never says that. It gives an answer for every scenario. Even in the *yissurin shel ahavah* scenario, one comes to that conclusion after much consideration. One doesn't simply say that only God knows the reason for my pain.

Rabbi Weinberg would often tell me that we can know and we must know why things happen to us.

There is a wonderful illustration of this in the book of Genesis.

Joseph was sold by his brothers and taken down to Egypt. He had not turned up for over twenty years. As far as they were concerned, he was dead and gone.

Now the brothers are faced with a famine in the land of Canaan and they, themselves, must go down to Egypt to find food. They enter the land and are immediately brought before the Egyptian viceroy (not knowing that he is in fact their brother Joseph). They explain to him that they are seeking food, and he accuses them of being spies. The only way he will allow them to go back home is if one of the brothers remains behind as a hostage, and if they promise to come back to Egypt with their youngest brother.

Troubles clearly are coming upon them. They are dealing with the most powerful man in the world, and he obviously has it in for them. What is the response of these great men in such a time of difficulty?

It is immediate and unequivocal. They say to each other, "We are guilty in that we saw our brother's pain and did not listen. And so this trouble has befallen us" *(Genesis 38:21).*

There is no discussion of how to respond in a pragmatic sense. Do they talk the viceroy out of it? Do they pay him off? Their first and foremost response is a purely spiritual one. We are in trouble and therefore it must be a message from God. What could the message be? It is obvious to all of them — we sold our brother into slavery of our own freewill and now this Egyptian is demanding another brother by force. Measure for measure. The hand of Providence is clear. And the brothers are quick to read it correctly and respond to it.

It is clear and obvious from the Talmud and from the response of Joseph's brothers that the Torah believes we can know the reason painful things happen to us, and if we want to respond properly, we must turn our attention towards understanding.

Far from being a horrible thought, this is actually an incredibly empowering concept.

If, as discussed earlier, hardship comes to teach us how to grow, then we need to know in which area God wants us to grow — otherwise we cannot grow in the way that we are being guided. Rabbi Weinberg often said to me, "Why would God send us a message — but send it in Chinese? If you had an important message to send your children, so important that you felt it necessary to put them through pain in order to get it across, would you send it in a foreign language?"

Imagine that a parent sends his child to his room and when the child asks why, he says he's not going to tell him and the child won't be able to figure it out, either. It would be completely pointless. It would be a form of torture for a child to be reprimanded without being given any opportunity to identify the mistake and correct it.

I have sometimes heard people say that pain is not really a message, but rather a medium — that the pain, in and of itself, corrects us. We don't need to figure out the reason and learn from it; we just need to go through the difficult experience, and in doing so we will change.

Whilst there may be instances where this is true, it cannot and must not be said as a blanket statement about Judaism's perspective on pain. If this is the purpose for all pain, it means that God is denying us the freewill to change what we have done; rather He does it for us. The concept that we make mistakes and God corrects them through pain sounds like another religion far removed from our own. It applies only after the process of considering one's deeds has been undertaken.

In Judaism, freewill is a given. We are not robots; we are independent beings. God will not force us to change; but He will give us the opportunity and guidance to choose for ourselves. Pain, in general, cannot be something that changes us automatically, for that would mean God changing *us* rather than us changing *ourselves*. There may be a place for pain as a means to eradicate the residue of mistakes that have already been dealt with. But on the whole, pain is a conduit to direct us to make our own changes. In order to do so, we must understand the message and make the decisions accordingly.

The fact that we can understand our own pain and change accordingly is incredibly empowering. Because if God is doing something we cannot understand, then we are mere puppets. We have no control of the outcome. In that case, pain is simply a roller coaster ride and all we can do is hold on tight. If, however, we can understand what is happening, then we can change it. We made the mess and we can clean it up. We are masters of our own destiny.

I do not say this in a flippant fashion. For a father to subject his children to pain, there must be something very wrong. And you do not correct something very wrong in an easy and quick way. We can find an example in the book of Esther. The Jews wrongly attended the banquet of King Achashveirosh. It was inappropriate for them to have participated in the lavish party of an evil man. Not long after, Haman is appointed Prime Minister of Persia and given the king's signet ring. He now has not only the will but also the power to bring about the utter annihilation of the Jewish people.

The Rabbis tell us that when Haman received the royal seal, the Jews of Shushan understood immediately what they had done wrong. They fasted three days and returned to God. In response, God overturned the decree for their destruction. It required a gargantuan response from the Jewish people — but it worked. So too, with a similar level of response and responsibility, it seems to me that an individual can overturn a personal decree.

It might require levels of commitment such that it is unlikely to happen in most cases; but I believe it's important to appreciate, nevertheless, that it can be done. Moses, for example, prayed 515 times in order to be allowed to enter the Land of Israel — something God had clearly decreed would not happen. After 515 times, God told him to stop praying, because if he prayed any more, God would be forced, so to speak, to allow him to enter, something that would not be right for the Jewish People as a whole. Decrees can be changed. It's only a matter of how much we care to do so — and being that most of us would not pray 15 times, let alone 515 times for something like this, we are unlikely to overturn decrees once they are set in place, but that does not mean we are not able to do so.

It is possible to understand and to change and to take away the pain. We are in complete control of our destiny. This is the reality of freewill. And it's a beautiful thing.

Let me not be misunderstood. Most of the time, pain is a unique message for the individual himself. A number of people may experience the same pain, the same disease or calamity, but it might be a very different message for each. The message is always intensely personal. As such, although a person can understand a message that is given to him, he can in no way assume to understand the message given to another. He can speculate, he can advise, but he can never "know" the reason. Only the person going through the pain can decide the purpose for it — for only he or she can know him or herself well enough to know the mistakes that have been made and where they have stemmed from. Pain is an incredibly intimate and personal (and beautiful) aspect of God's relationship with us, one to which others are not necessarily privy. It is not for anyone else to judge why another person might be suffering. It is for others to support and love, not judge why.

At the time of the prophets, things were different. When a person was ill, instead of going to a doctor, he would go to a prophet who would tell him via divine inspiration the reason for his illness. Without prophets today, we have only ourselves to rely on. One might feel this is a daunting task, but I do believe that we can reach the same understanding.

Usually, the more daunting a task, the greater the level of Heavenly assistance we receive. A person in the time of the prophets would not have been able to figure it out for himself — for he did not need to do so. I would suggest that perhaps we, who can be seen as "spiritual orphans," are given more assistance.

There is no question that it's important to get advice from others on the issue, to discuss with friends, spouses, and certainly Rabbis. They can give advice and guidance and they can help confirm conclusions that we might reach. But ultimately, in the absence of prophets, the individual has no real choice other than trying his very best to draw his own conclusion.

When Elana and I understood this, we felt infinitely better. We could understand what God was saying to us and we could change. And we could turn the decree around.

Why then, you might ask, did she die? As I have explained, that is a question that only I can answer for myself — and I have my answers. I have shared much and will share more, but this far I am unwilling to go. Suffice it to say, it poses no philosophical problem for me. It poses pain, but not doubt. And, thankfully, no guilt. Only God is perfect, not me, nor any of us. Elana is in a beautiful place, taking pleasure in how much she achieved during her short lifetime. I and my family are doing very well. Things might have been different, but they were not. At the end of it all, though, 'what ifs' are never helpful; things are always just right the way that they are.

How Do You Do It?

I t's all very well to say that you can know, but how do you go about figuring it out? What is the mechanism for doing so? Let me start with an idea that was of significant help to Elana and me in getting this concept into our bones.

I often find that people are great at seeing where God 'is not' in our lives. But we are not so great at seeing just where He 'is.' When things go wrong, we usually ask, "Where was God? Why did He allow this to happen to us?" Rarely, however, when things go right, do we give Him the credit for working things out.

How often will we give God the credit when a business deal goes well or when we find what we were looking for in the first store we enter, or even when we easily find a parking space? It's only fair that if God is going to take the rap when problems arise, He should also get the credit when things go well. He's either in control or not. It can't be that He's in control when things go wrong, but we're in control when they go right!

It stands to reason that if we have a distorted and unfair picture of God's involvement in our lives, we will have difficulty putting into perspective that which causes us pain.

It's like a parent-child relationship. The extent to which the child feels confident of his parent's love is the extent to which he can be accepting of his rebuke. A child who doubts his parent's love will respond negatively to any reprimand. But a child who feels a deep sense of love from his parents will surely respect them when they make decisions which cause him pain. As long as he knows that they're on his side, he will be able to handle whatever they throw at him!

The same is true of our relationship with God. If we are to relate to God properly during difficult times we need to know that He is on our side. And the time to feel that God is on our side is when things are good. If we develop that feeling during the good times, we will have a 'friend' during the hard times. But if we fail to feel God's love when all is going our way, we will certainly not feel it when we go through pain.

When Elana first became ill, Rabbi Weinberg gave us a suggestion that really helped us focus on God's love for us. He suggested that on

Friday night, we tell "*hashgachah* stories." Stories of how, during the past week, we saw God's hand in our lives. It might have been something as simple as finding a parking space right outside the store or being late for a train and finding that the train was also late. "Look for God in your life and you will find Him," was the principle. And it worked wonders for us. It has long been an integral part of our Friday night experience. Our children love finding stories in the week where God was clearly a part of their lives (and the treat they get for coming up with a story certainly helps!) This gets the whole family in touch with the fact that God is here with us on a daily basis.

As a result of thirteen years of doing this, each of us have become a family that very much recognizes God's direct and ongoing involvement in our lives. Over and over again, events will happen during the week and our children (even the very young ones) will point out the *hashgachah* in what happened. If money blows in through our front door, the first thing our children would shout out is, "Wow, *hashgachah*!" It's not a random happening and it's not luck. It's God giving us a gift.

I want to share my two favorite examples: My sister-in-law needed to get a train home one day. She put her money into the ticket machine, but just as she did, she realized she did not have enough cash. Here she was, stuck in Central London, where she didn't know a soul! She pushed the cancel button to get her money back, and when she picked up the change, she saw the ticket machine had given her back more than she had originally put in! And it was exactly the correct amount of money for her ticket!

But my favorite story of all came from my son, Elkana, who was five years old at the time. One Friday night, he related that he had just opened a bottle of fizzy drink at the table. It had been shaken up, so it squirted out all over the place. But, by *hashgachah*, it was pointing in the right direction. Not a drop went on him. It went all over his little sister instead!

Hashgachah stories are a way of bringing an awareness of God into your daily life. The more you see God's hand in everything, the easier it will be to see His hand and feel His love in the pain, too.

These stories will help put you in the frame of mind that when pain comes, instead of becoming angry and frustrated that life is not going your way, you can, as the Rabbis say, examine your deeds and understand what God is saying to you from a peaceful and comfortable place. With *hashgachah* stories as the backdrop to life's challenges, let's discuss how one actually goes about finding a message in the pain.

A friend, Rabbi Moshe Mayerfeld, gave the analogy of sitting across the room from someone who's trying to signal something to you. They mouth what they are trying to say, make signs, jump up and down, and you just don't get the point. Now take the same scenario with your spouse or a close friend across the room. They can wink an eye or wave a hand and you immediately get it. The closer you are to someone, the easier it is to understand the message they are communicating.

So, too, with God. For those who are close, the meaning of the message comes relatively easily. For those of us who are a little farther away, we have to work a little harder.

As with anything in life, however, practice makes perfect. I can teach you to play tennis in ten minutes — forehand, backhand, serve, smash, lob, spin, the works… But now let's see you get the ball over the net! There are no magic formulas that will work immediately. You just have to have patience and give it time and effort. And you'll get frustrated and feel you're not progressing at first — as with anything new. But I guarantee this — persevere as you would with tennis, and in a relatively short period of time, you'll start to get the hang of it.

Chapter 6
Count Your Blessings

I still remember Elana waking up in the middle of the night, a few days before she died. She could hardly speak, due to her serious lack of breath, but she desperately wanted to communicate. Finally, when she got the words out, she simply wanted to say, while beaming her big smile, "I am so incredibly blessed." I can tell you for sure that she didn't feel this way before she got cancer. Her mindset changed during the illness.

I often use the following example when I teach a class on this topic.

I ask a person how he would feel if he just won $10 million in the lottery. Would he have a big grin on his face? Would he be skipping down the street, singing as he went? Most people answer that they surely would.

Okay, I continue, we're doing some medical research and we need a fresh leg to experiment on. We're willing to pay you $10 million for one of your legs. It's a painless operation, over in an hour, and you'll hop out of the hospital $10 million richer. We'll even throw in the latest prosthetic as a freebie. There may be the odd person who would take me up on the offer, but most people decline.

Okay, I continue, you won't take $10 million for one of your legs? That means you possess something more valuable than a mere $10 million. In fact, you have two of them! And you wouldn't give up your arms either, nor your eyes, nor your tongue, nor your hearing, nor your emotions, nor your independence... The list goes on. In fact, when you add it all up, every single human being — no matter what his circumstance — has gifts that he himself would value at billions. We are all billionaires! And most of us are miserable billionaires, at that!

It doesn't make sense. If we would skip down the street for just $10 million of lottery money, why then are we not skipping down the street for being multi-billionaires?

There is a classic example of this in the book of Esther again. Haman, the evil Prime Minister of the Persian Empire, is riding high on the crest of not just a wave, but a tidal wave. He is one of the wealthiest men in the world. He is arguably the most powerful man in the world; and respected and honored by all. He has ten wonderful sons who idolize him and a wife who adores him. The whole world bows to him — all, that is, except for one man, Mordechai the Jew. And so, Haman is miserable. He says to Zeresh, his wife, that all his wealth, all his honor, all his power means nothing to him, as long as Mordechai does not bow down *(Esther 5:11–13)*. He has it all, but really he has nothing. He is so obsessed with Mordechai that he can think of nothing else. But Mordechai is not his problem. If Mordechai would have bowed down to him, you can be sure he would have found something else to irritate him — his sick hamster or his inability to play the mouth organ. It doesn't matter what it is. When your thoughts are about what you don't have, something along the way will make you miserable.

Here's what happened with Elana. Prior to her cancer, her mind was buzzing – like so many people. Life seemed so busy, so many kids, so much to do, so many challenges, problems, difficulties…

Then she got cancer. And all of that became very petty. Again, like most of us, nonsense had distracted her. But unlike most of us, she awoke to a deep realization of the truth of that. And as the nonsense all faded away, she realized what was important – her husband, her children, life itself, her fleeting time in this world, her friends, her happiness. Her focus changed and she awoke to a new reality. Nothing changed and yet everything changed. She had nothing new in her life and yet her life was suddenly so, so rich.

Deepening one's understanding about the issue is likely to provide that insight ultimately, but bottom line, insights that change us are a gift from God and when we are ready for them, He will provide them for us. For Elana, her illness made her ready.

I was granted a particular insight in this area soon after Elana passed away. I used to wake up in the morning and actively count my blessings. I had worked out my fifteen greatest gifts in life and I would go through them one by one, thanking God for each of them. Of course, Elana was high on the list. I woke up the day after Elana passed away and started with my list. I reached Elana and my heart suddenly sank. I could no longer thank God for this blessing because it had been wrenched away from me. In that moment, my insight came. Was Elana no longer a blessing because she was no longer here? Had she not blessed my life for twelve years? Was I not a completely different human being because of her? Was I not everything because of her? I was shocked that I had even considered taking her off the list. Instead, I thanked God for twelve years with this most wonderful of women and as I did so I realized this: If God was to give me the option right now of never having met Elana and hence having avoided the pain of losing her — I would not hesitate to decline. I could easily complain that God did not give me more time with her. But why would I want to do that when instead I could thank God for the incredible and eternal blessing that she had brought to my life? As I write this, even thirteen years later, I feel no less grateful for all of the years that I had her for.

Some people work on happiness for years and remain depressed. Others, like Elana, don't work on it at all and yet awaken to a new understanding. It's not a matter of the effort you put into it, it's just a matter of recognizing the understanding when it comes your way. God is sending us insights about this all the time, we just need to look out for them and notice them when they come our way. Elana noticed – and found deep and lasting happiness.

Like I have said, we are all so blessed. If we are open to the potential of seeing it that way.

From this newfound sense of perspective came something that we did and enjoyed doing until the very end of her life.

Elana and I did what we called "Thank You, *Hashem's*." Every day we would try to do this five times at regular intervals and ideally together — face to face or over the phone. If we couldn't do it together, we would do it separately.

We would thank God for five good things that had happened during the last few hours. Let's say we would do this first at 10 a.m., so this might be how it would go — "Thank You, *Hashem*, for a delicious breakfast this morning and thank You for loving me." Ideally, we would try to make the pleasure more real by describing it and savoring it with each other — the corn flakes were crunchy and tasted nutritious. I enjoyed the sensation of crunching them between my teeth and chewing them. The milk was cold and felt good in my throat. The sugar gave me a sweet sensation.

"Thank You, *Hashem*, for giving me a wonderful two minutes with my son this morning and thank You for loving me. I loved the way that he smiled at me so warmly and I was able to give him the answer he needed for his homework and he went off to school so excited and full of joy. I loved his happiness and his energy so early in the morning, and thank You for loving me."

"Thank You, *Hashem*, for the cold fresh air this morning. I loved the way I felt more awake and alive when I went out, the way that the cold air felt fresh and energizing, the crispness of the cold winter's day."

We would do five of these "Thank You, *Hashems*" five times a day. It was exhilarating.

At the end of a day of chemotherapy, we found ourselves thanking God for the wonderful walk we had on Hampstead Heath instead of complaining about the horrors of the disease and its treatment. Those were indeed precious moments.

Another Cancer Patient

I once met a cancer patient who was in remission. It was well before my own experiences with Elana.

He came to me after a class in which I was talking about some of the above ideas and told me that he very much related to what I was talking about. He was a cancer patient and had fairly recently been undergoing serious chemotherapy in a hospital in New York City. He said that he had been so sick from the chemo that he couldn't see properly, couldn't hear properly, couldn't walk without feeling dizzy. He was throwing up all the time. He happened to be in a room facing a busy street and was able to look outside and see people hurrying past. Everyone seemed to be in a big hurry to get somewhere, but they didn't look particularly happy. In fact, he felt they actually looked quite miserable.

He said that if he could have, he would have screamed out of the window, "Idiots, why are you so miserable? You can see properly, you can walk without being dizzy. You are not throwing up constantly. You are not battling a terminal illness. You should be skipping. You should be dancing. You should be singing."

He swore to himself that if he ever made it into remission, he would make sure that he danced. And so he did. Not long after, the chemo had done its job and he was released from hospital. He said to me that for two whole weeks, he had sung; he had danced; he had skipped down the street without a care in the world.

"Now, Rabbi," he told me, "I am back to being one of them!"

There was something I decided for myself, very soon after Elana died. I realized that I could lose my wife and be miserable. Or I could lose my wife and be happy. Losing my wife was something totally beyond my control. In my mind, God had made a good but painful decision for me. But happiness? That was within my own hands. I had choice. I could look in the direction of happiness and realize it had nothing to do with what happened to me in life. Or I could look in the direction of what I had lost and feel very sorry for myself. Losing my wife was something painful, but being unhappy would be something even worse. Why have two painful things happen to me when it only needed to be one? I made my choice and looked in the direction of happiness. And boy am I glad that I did.

I certainly wasn't happy all the time, but because my preference was happiness, it rose to the surface on a regular basis.

Happiness isn't a happening, it's a preference. People who genuinely prefer happiness will find it regularly. And will be less enthralled with the times that life doesn't seem worth living. I'm not sure it's possible to be happy all of the time. But I do believe that in preferring happiness it becomes the default position. And just like a ball filled with air that is pushed down into water will always rise to the surface, so too, happiness, even when lost, will always appear once again.

Chapter 7
Prayer

T he Jewish People believe that prayer has genuine power. God
listens to our prayers and takes them seriously. Prayer can
change reality.

One of the great challenges of an illness like secondary cancer —
though it applies to many other circumstances — is the feeling of lack
of control. You just don't know what's going on. The doctors don't
know what's going on; they don't really know if they can cure you —
and if they had to take a guess, they'd probably say they can't. It's all
doom and gloom and there is seemingly nothing you can do.

Well, let me tell you that there is very much something you can
do. You can pray. And it throws the ball back into your court. You
have, through your relationship with the Being Who controls all circumstances, the ability to turn things around — the ability to turn
anything around.

The more sincerity and commitment you are able to pray with,
the more you will feel that you really are involved, that you have
a say in the outcome. You are not just sitting and watching while
something bad happens to you. You are engaging life with a powerful tool.

Whether or not you end up winning is not what matters. What
matters is that you are involved, engaged, not a victim. You have a
friend who can help — and an omnipotent friend, at that.

How one should pray, modes of prayer, and tapping into the
power of prayer are issues that are beyond the scope of this particular book, but suffice it to say that prayer is, in and of itself, deeply
comforting.

God Is Not a Vending Machine

A number of people asked me how I felt about the fact that I prayed so much for Elana — and I really did — and yet my prayers were not answered. Not only did I pray, but hundreds and thousands of others poured out their hearts for Elana — and yet she died.

I have often heard people say in response to this question that God always answers our prayers, but sometimes His answer is "no." I don't believe this answer. I believe that prayer is much more powerful than that.

God's answer is always a positive answer. But sometimes the answer is positive in the way you asked for it, and sometimes the answer is positive in a way you didn't imagine.

I can't say that I came to this insight easily.

During *shivah*, I was really struggling to relate to the words we say three times in the morning service, "God is our savior. Our King will answer us on the day that we call" *(Psalms 20:10)*. The words began to bother me when I said them. They no longer made sense to me. I had called and called and called for almost three years. I had cried tropical rainstorms of tears — and I had not been answered. My wife had died.

I asked Rabbi Weinberg, my teacher, and he gave me an answer that, over time, felt very right to me. I was asking God to heal my wife. And He did. But not in the way I was looking for. The way He healed her was greater than anything I could have imagined. He healed her not physically, but spiritually, and I was and am envious of the spiritual health that she attained. A few days before she passed away, she said that for the first time in her life, she truly felt that God loved her. She had always known it, but had never been able to fully feel it. Now she did. She felt at one with God and at one with me. She felt at one with herself and she knew that life really is beautiful. While her body was as sick as a body can be, her soul was healthier than anyone I had ever met. Only two days before her passing, she told me that she would not swap places with anyone!

Why didn't God heal her soul and body, as well? It's a good question, but if I knew the full extent of God's ways — I would be God

Himself. And whilst I might be very much a part of Him, I am certainly not Him! So I don't know why both were not possible. (As I mentioned earlier, I feel that I know in terms of my own self why God did not heal my wife. I know where I was inadequate, and I don't judge myself for it. I am human like every one else. But from Elana's perspective, I have no clue as to why He didn't heal her in spite of my deficiencies. In other words, even if my actions did not merit her getting better, she was the one who was sick and surely her prayers and her *teshuva* had the ability to cure her also. Why did they not? Did she somehow fall short also? I don't believe that she did. In which case, it must be that God had a higher purpose and I don't suppose at all to even consider what that might be. But one thing I do know is that God *did* heal her! And if for some reason there had to be a choice between spiritual and physical health, I know which she would have chosen — and I also know which I like to think I would have had the strength to choose had our roles been reversed.

God answered when I called — just not with the answer I asked for. But God is not a vending machine. You don't just insert your prayer, push a button, and receive your Pepsi. Rather, God is a loving, caring Father with Whom we have a dynamic relationship. We pray. He listens, considers, and decides how best to respond, based on who we are and what we need. And His answer is always positive.

Growth from Prayer

I do feel that every prayer I said for my wife changed me. It changed my relationship with her. It changed my relationship with myself, and, of course, it changed my relationship with God. In my mind, no prayer was wasted. Each accomplished its mission — that of making me a little more Godly. Each prayer softened my heart and humbled me. I am a very different person today because of the intensity of the prayers I said for my wife during her illness. And I am so grateful for what it has given me.

Judaism maintains that we are here in this world to get closer to God. Through our prayers, Elana got closer to God; I got closer to

God; those around us also got closer to God; the thousands who prayed for her got closer to God. The details of the situation were difficult, very difficult. It is not the way that any of us wanted it to happen. But the results were those that we were looking for. Our prayers were answered in an incredibly positive way.

I don't expect to understand every aspect of what happens in the world. I don't tell my kids everything, and God doesn't tell me everything, either. But this I do know: I pray and He answers. I might not always fully understand His answer, but it is always a loving "yes." And I will always be a better person because of it.

Chapter 8
Bitachon, Trust

Trusting in God is probably the key to it all. A person who feels that God is on his side, loving him and doing what is best for him, should feel comfortable with any circumstance that comes his way.

Easy to say, rabbi.

It's true that for the most part, trust in God does not just happen. People don't go to bed one night feeling that God is out to get them and wake up the next day confident that they can rely on Him — no matter what illegal substances they might imbibe.

So how do you do it?

Firstly, trust is a feeling. You can intellectualize all you want, but if you don't feel confident that someone will catch you at the bottom of the ladder, you aren't going to jump.

There's an old story of the atheist who falls off a cliff one thousand feet high. He grabs onto a single twig five hundred feet down. He looks up to heaven and figures he doesn't have all that many options.

"Is there anybody up there?" he asks.

"Yes, it's me, God," comes the response.

"Thank God for that," the atheist replies. "Please God, help me. I'll do anything."

"Of course, my son. But I have just one request to make."

"Anything, God," replies the atheist.

"I will save you, my child," says God, "but you have to trust Me first. Let go of the twig and I will catch you."

The atheist looks down at the rocks five hundred feet below and looks up again.

"Is there anybody else up there?"

The point is clear. You can know there's a God intellectually, but ultimately, it's the feeling that counts. A person can switch from being an atheist to a believer in a single moment if he or she were to have a clear experience of God. But trusting in God is something different.

The Seven Elements of Bitachon, Trust

According to the tenth century classic, *Chovos HaLevavos* (Duties of the Heart), written by Rabbeinu Bechaya, there are seven elements involved in trust in God *(Shaar HaBitachon, ch. 2)*. If you feel all seven, your trust will be complete. But it's not an all-or-nothing proposition. Any level of any of these elements will help you feel some sense of trust. I am not using the order of the original book, but rather, an order put together by Rabbi Weinberg. I am also paraphrasing Rabbeinu Bechaya's words in the way that Rabbi Weinberg explained the concepts to me.

Remember that:

1. God loves me with a love that is deeper than the love I have for my children or that my parents have for me. In fact, it is deeper than the love of any parent for any child. In fact, if one combined into a single intense emotion all of the love of every parent for every child since time began, God's love for me would be deeper and more intense. God loves me as a unique individual. I am His special, sweet little child. I personally imagine God holding me in His arms, smiling at me, as I do with my children, enveloping me in His love.

2. God knows my every need, my every challenge, and my every problem. He knows what I feel, what I think, what concerns me, what worries me. He knows exactly what's on my mind and He knows it constantly. He doesn't forget about me, not even for a moment. Nothing slips past Him. He "thinks" about me and my problems 24/7. During Elana's illness, I thought, He knows

the location of every cancer cell in her body. No rogue cell can slip by unnoticed and start growing on its own. He is fully aware and cognizant of all that is going on. He is in complete control and charge of every single cell of her body and takes no time off. He also knows what is worrying me — what's on my mind. He knows my concerns and my fears. He knows my hopes and my aspirations. He knows exactly what I'm feeling, exactly what I want. Whenever I might choose to speak to Him, at any time of day, He is listening and taking me seriously, before I even begin.

3. God has the power to do anything. There is nothing that I need that He cannot provide me; nothing I am lacking that is not His to give. He is able to solve all my problems and solve them immediately. He is not only able to solve current problems; He is fully capable of preventing any new problems from arising. In the context of Elana, I was always sure that He had the ability to take away every single cancer cell instantly. I would think, He can change the whole situation around in a moment. And it's not difficult for Him to do so. My wife could jump out of bed tomorrow, free of cancer, as though nothing had ever happened. Whether or not He will do that is another issue. But He certainly CAN do so.

4. Nothing else has any power. There is nothing that works independent of God. Nothing, no matter how small, can or does happen without His full approval and intimate involvement. He does not give His power to other forces. He remains in full control at all times. There is no cancer; there is just God. There is no chemotherapy; there is just God. Cancer cells do not grow by themselves; God makes them grow. And there is not a single one that can grow without God's command for it to do so. God and cancer are not adversaries. They are partners. No treatment can circumvent His will. If He wishes the treatment to work, then it will, and if He does not, then it will not.

5. God has done so much for me until now. He has given me life. He has given me freewill. He makes my heart beat. He makes the blood run through my body. He gives me air to breathe, food to eat. He provides warmth. He has given me intelligence, emotions,

time in this world, eyes, legs, arms, ears... You name it, He has done it. He has a track record of complete and utter unwarranted goodness to me. Given how He has related to me up to now, surely anything I need or want is a small thing in comparison. It's like asking my father to give me a dime to make a phone call. It's a small-time request compared to what He has already done. If He did not give it to me, I would be absolutely shocked. Taking the cancer away is nothing compared to making my heart constantly pump just enough oxygen to my brain for the past forty-eight years. And He did that without my even asking. Surely, if I ask Him, He will take my prayer very seriously.

6. God's love is unconditional. It is not dependent on my actions or my way of life. Like a good parent, He loves me no matter what. Even when I stumble and make some very big mistakes, He still loves me. Even when I completely ignore Him, He loves me. His love is with me no matter who I am or what I do. Despite all my imperfections, I can feel secure that God is still backing me. Yes, God would like me to be great. Yes, His expectations for me are massive — because of what I can accomplish with the soul He has given me. But those expectations are purely based on His desire to give to me. He expects from me because He wants me to find fulfillment. And so, I could waste all my potential and He might still make Elana better, just because He loves me. And if He did not make her better, it would still only be that because of His love for me, He knows that this is what is best for me.

7. Like any good parent, God will always give me just what I need. Life will not always be exactly what I want to it be. He may not give me what I think will be good for me. But He will always give me what is really good for me. No matter what I am going through, it is exactly what I need to be going through at that moment. Whatever God might have in store for me, the road this illness is taking us down is a road we need to traverse. And wherever that road might lead, its destination is where we need to get to.

For me, this final point creates the greatest sense of trust and security. No matter what I am going through — no matter how 'bad' or painful it may seem, I know that it is for my ultimate good.

During the difficult months after my wife's passing, this point was always one that I would fall back on. God gives me what I need. This is what I need. It is not bad. It is good. It will bring me closer to Him — if I choose for it to do so.

Turning your attention in the direction of these ideas is helpful. It's helpful to remember them — not to 'try' to feel them, not to force yourself. We human beings don't change when we force ourselves. Simply look in their direction and see if you feel differently. Elana and I used to consider them ten times a day at regular intervals. We found doing it together fun, as we would alternate the elements and talk about what each one meant to us.

You need to be patient. You need to trust that trust will come. It is my belief that Torah works. The Rabbis know what they are talking about. There is amazing wisdom in Rabbeinu Bachya's *Chovos Ha-Levavos*. Yet it does require patience. These are the ideas you need to know and when you know them from your own soul, you will find a deep and lasting trust in God.

Chapter 9
It's All for the Best

The Rabbis tell the story of Rabbi Akiva who was travelling with a donkey, a candle, and a rooster *(Berachos 60b)*. He went into a city to find a place to sleep and was turned away. "Everything God does is for the best" he said and went to spend the night in a field outside the city. His lamp blew out in the wind. "Everything God does is for the best," he said once again. His rooster was mauled by a fox. "Everything God does is for the best," he repeated. Then his donkey was eaten by a lion. Once again, Rabbi Akiva repeated the mantra, "Everything God does is for the best."

When he awoke in the morning, he ventured into the city and realized that bandits had attacked it during the night, capturing many people. Had he found a place to stay, he would probably have also been captured. Had the bandits noticed a lamp in a field nearby or heard his donkey or rooster, he might also have been in trouble. Instead, his life was saved by all the 'bad' things that happened to him.

There is an important note that must go with this story. If God had wanted to save Rabbi Akiva from the bandits, surely He could have let him find a nice room in the city for himself, his lamp, his rooster, and his donkey and let him sleep through the night unmolested. If God is all powerful, then He can do things in a way that is more, rather than less, comfortable. Rabbi Akiva might have been saved, but he still went through pain. Why could he not have been saved in a painless way?

I think that there was a message here for Rabbi Akiva. Yes, he was a great enough man that he should be saved in a miraculous way. But he did not merit an open miracle of staying in the city and being saved during a rampage. There was something lacking in him that God was trying to point out to him. Yes, it was good — for it is always good. But it was painful also, and in pain there is always a lesson.

In the *Amidah* that Jews say every day of the year, it states that God is *gomel chasadim tovim* — He does good deeds of kindness. This seems, at first glance, to be redundant. Surely deeds of kindness are all "good." How could a kindness be bad?

The answer is that you can be kind and nice to someone — but that is not necessarily what is best for them. People will sometimes benefit more from painful experiences than nice ones. This is not for us to decide. We need to be nice, give people pleasant experiences and leave the painful ones for God to work out.

There remains, however, a question. The *Amidah* says that God is a doer of "good kindnesses." This does not seem to be correct. Almost every day in almost every person's life, there will be goodness that does not feel so kind. Goodness is unarguable — for we do not see a complete picture — but whether a circumstance *feels* good to us or not is something we can certainly judge. And very often it does not. So how can we say that God does "good kindnesses?"

I think the answer lies in the context of the phrase. This is in the *Amidah* — we are praising God in prayer. We are talking about Who God is in real terms; what He is in essence. In essence, God is a being Who does "good kindnesses." That is His nature, so to speak. But in the reality of this world, He is not always able to do that. He has given us freewill, and if He is to maintain that, He must sometimes respond to our decisions with pain. It hurts Him, so to speak, much more than it hurts us. But it is what He needs to do. It is not the way He would choose to act, but given the greater good of freewill, it is the way that He must act.

So too the Rabbis would say "Everything God does is for the best" immediately upon something 'bad' happening.

When we first heard of Elana's cancer, I found it very difficult to say this to myself. In fact, Elana was able to say it much sooner than I. The whole experience caused me to examine what the Rabbis mean by this phrase, and I discovered an insight that has made it possible for me to say it very easily nowadays.

I used to understand the idea as follows. When something bad happens to you, take a moment to remind yourself that God has a plan; that He knows what he's doing and he's not making a mistake. It looks bad, but that's only how it looks on the surface. You'll look back one day and realize just how good it was.

That's how I used to understand the purpose of saying this phrase — simply to remind us that God is in control at a time that one might panic and forget.

Now I think that the idea is much, much deeper.

We live in a neutral world. Everything has the potential to go one way or the other. A gun can kill, but it can also protect. Medicine can heal, but too much of it or given in the wrong circumstances, can make you sick. Computers can enhance our lives – and they can help us to waste our lives. Nuclear energy can light up cities — and destroy civilizations. Even something like Torah — a book of wisdom for life — the Rabbis tell us can be an elixir of life or an elixir of death. Nothing is good and nothing is bad. All is neutral depending on how it is used. Things become good or bad depending on human choice — they do not start out that way.

The same is true of events in our lives. Our response is that which defines which way they will go, whether an event is something that will bring more good feeling to our lives or bring us more problems.

All events, as such, are completely neutral.

You win the lottery. There is a lot of good there. You can support your family. You can enjoy God's beautiful world. You can give money to charity. You can be free to pursue meaning and wisdom. That's all great. But with money comes other things.

From now on, how will you know who is sincere in their friendship for you? How will you be able to trust people? You will become much more of a target for robbery. You will be more likely to worry and think about losing your money now that you have it. I remember once talking to a man who lives in a forty-million-pound house on a beautiful road in London. He was telling me about how wonderful his security was — he had dogs and he had cameras throughout his house, as well as all the way up his driveway. (Before the cameras, he was once attacked in his driveway and he and his wife were beaten up before the thieves ran off with his money.) I told him that I have no cameras. I have no dogs. I open my door to strangers without fear. Is the money really worth it? And he wasn't sure.

Money has its blessings but also its curses. It's just that the blessings are more immediately obvious and the curses are a little more subtle.

The same is true of 'bad' things. Let's take a person's house burning down. It's easy to see the bad elements of that, but what about the good? Well, there are many possibilities. Maybe it will give him more humility — something worth much more than a mere house. Maybe he will have to spend time with his family in less spacious surroundings and will have the opportunity to get closer to them as a result. Or maybe even just the challenge itself will be something that brings them closer together. Maybe it will put life and possessions into perspective for him. There are many positive elements one could focus on, depending on the circumstances. And the choice is always ours to make.

"Everything God does is for the best" is a reminder, at a time of seeming challenge, that there is good in this also. It's a reminder for a person to choose. It's almost a person challenging himself — this is good, now go and find out why.

At the moment of a new and difficult experience in life, there is a choice to be made — will I look for the good or will I wallow in the frustration and upset? Do I want to find good, or am I satisfied with how it seems on the surface.

Saying "Everything God does is for the best" is simply a form of orienting oneself. Let me be open to the good. And when a person is open to the good, he will always find it. Because the good is not in the circumstance, it is in the choice itself. "Everything God does is for the best" then is not simply a reminder, it is the choice itself. Not 'this is for the best,' rather 'this can be for the best if I choose to see it that way.' It's in my hands…

The story is told of the great sage of two thousand years ago, Hillel the Elder. He was walking into his town and heard a great commotion coming from one of the houses. People were screaming and crying and clearly something terrible had happened. He could not hear where the cries were coming from, but he said he could be certain they were not coming from his own house. It is usually understood to mean that Hillel knew that God would not allow something 'bad' like this to happen in his home.

The Shelah *(Asarah Maamaros, 5)*, the great 16th Century Rabbi, asks a question, however. We know that no one is perfect. Even Hillel must have made mistakes in his life. How could he be so sure that God would not allow something painful to happen in his home? And even if he could be sure, Hillel is known in the Talmud for his great humility. This does not sound overly humble — to suggest that he was so righteous that nothing could happen to him or his household?

The Shelah answers as follows: There was no question in Hillel's mind that painful experiences could happen in his home. But what he knew was that if something did, his household would surely not respond this way. He was a man versed in the art of "Everything God does is for the best." And he knew that it had rubbed off on the members of his household. In the same way as he would not shout and cry, no matter what happened, he was confident that they would act in the same manner. When 'bad' happened, they would surely not scream and wail. They would say "Everything God does is for the best" and start finding the good.

Screaming and wailing could not come from his household. So he could be sure that whatever had happened had not been in his home.

As an aside, it's interesting to note that Rabbi Akiva's Rabbi was Nachum Ish Gamzu. His name derives from the phrase that he would say all the time, 'Gam zu letovah — also this is for the good.' This is a very slightly different phrase from the one that Rabbi Akiva used. I heard the difference explained as follows: Nachum Ish Gamzu's level of trust in God was greater than that of his student, Rabbi Akiva. For Rabbi Akiva, as in the story mentioned, good would eventually arise from what seemed like something bad right now. It just required patience. Nachum Ish Gamzu took it a step further. Not that good would arise in the future but that it is good right now — even though it seems bad. Nachum Ish Gamzu did not need to wait until he saw the good, his conviction of God's goodness was so strong and so deep that he knew it was good immediately, even though he had yet to see it play itself out. Rabbi Akiva said, "I know I will see the good of this in the future." Nachum Ish Gamzu said, "I know the goodness of this right now." It is a subtle, yet significant distinction.

Conclusion

The title of this book is *Why Bad Things Don't happen to Good People*. I hope what I have written has shown this to be true for you, the reader. As I said in my introduction, why bad things happen to good people is probably the oldest philosophical question that mankind has asked. I would not be so presumptuous, therefore, to suggest that I have answered it in its entirety. However, I do hope that in what I have written, I been able to provide understanding such that it will significantly soften the question in the eyes of those who are concerned by it.

We live in a world of pain and there is absolutely nothing we can do to circumvent that reality. We can hide from pain, we can experience pain with or without dignity, or we can appreciate that pain is one of God's greatest and most versatile gifts to humanity. It allows us to make meaningful choices about how we want to live our lives. It offers us the opportunity of independence. It shakes us out of apathy and into reality. And it pushes us to achieve and accomplish in a way that we otherwise never would.

In fact, just about the only downside of pain is that it hurts. But even that downside is limited inasmuch as the hurt is always only temporary.

As a society, we need to afford pain its rightful place. Running from it, as we often do, is not a path that will lead to happiness. I'm certainly not suggesting to go looking for pain, but when it comes, let's try to learn to treat it as a friend. I hope that the ideas contained within this book will contribute to your doing so. Elana left me with many gifts, but this was her greatest. It is to her that I once again give credit for all I have written — may her memory be a blessing.

Part Two

Finding Light in the Darkness

Our Story

Where Did We Come From?

E lana and I came from very different backgrounds. She grew up in Allentown, Pennsylvania, in a home with strong Torah values. Her family was steeped in *chesed* and deeply involved in the community. She loved going to synagogue from a very early age. She enjoyed learning. She would help others whenever and wherever she could. From the minute she became cognizant of the world, her focus was straight and unswerving: to serve her Creator in the best way possible.

I lived a very different life.

I grew up in Liverpool, and while my family was strongly Jewish, they lived a much more secular lifestyle. I won't bore you with the nitty-gritty, but at seventeen years of age, I found myself living with a cousin of mine and a black drug addict friend of his called Ray, and, for a short time, Ray's dealer, Johnny.

The four of us flatmates lived in Lark Lane, a very trendy area of Liverpool, while my parents had moved six thousand miles away to Los Angeles.

The drug that killed Ray in the end was heroin, "smack" as it was referred to — or, if you came from Liverpool, "smach." I often came home from high school to find Ray sprawled on the couch, his eyes wide open but only the whites were visible.

I must say that Ray was good to me. He realized I was a young, unworldly Jewish boy and took it as his personal mission to toughen me up. Many a time, he'd jump on me and see how far he could twist my arm behind my back before I begged for mercy. Looking at it from an outsider's point of view, it might sound a little strange — but there was method in his madness and I always appreciated his 'training sessions.'

I remember once, when my jacket was stolen from my car in broad daylight, he insisted that we chase after the thieves. We (read: he) caught them, and I, the little Jewish boy, sat terrified in the car while he 'sorted them out.' I got my jacket back at least.

It was at times like this when I wondered what life was all about and why exactly we were here. But I never took my inquiries any further.

But when I did start searching, I realized I had been given a head start. I attended a Jewish school — by chance much more than design. It was a secular Jewish school and over 50 percent of the student body was not Jewish (today it is 90 percent), but it had a Jewish identity nevertheless. Jewish studies were mandatory, and when I was sixteen, a rabbi came into my class on the first day of the new term. Surprisingly, he asked a question that to me had nothing whatsoever to do with Judaism. He asked our mixed and mixed-up class whether we believed in God. As someone who prided himself as a rational scientist (I was hoping one day to become an astronaut) I decidedly did not, and was unashamed to say so. "C'mon, Rabbi, these are modern times! Big Bang, Evolution, Existentialism — get with it, mate," was my general approach.

However, this rabbi was built of different stuff. He was undaunted by our Atheism and not ready to be bullied by the intellectual arrogance we represented. He said he could prove to us that there was a God and intended to do so over the next few weeks. He also said that he would prove that this God authored every letter of the Torah.

Well, just his willingness to take on such a tall order earned him some level of respect in our eyes, and we were generally ready to hear what he had to say.

However, after a few classes things changed for me.

He argued his points well and, to my own ears, my responses seemed weak. I tried to tell myself that he was well-rehearsed and expertly trained, but I was shaken. I couldn't pride myself on my scientific approach to life and then go ahead and be dishonest in my approach to God. The bottom line was that this rabbi was making way too much sense for my liking, and I took the only course of action I could. I refused to attend any more of his classes.

After a good bit of back and forth, and strong discussions with the headmaster, I was given an exemption from Jewish studies — much to the chagrin of the rabbi and the envy of my classmates.

That should have been that, and I should never have met Elana, but God had other plans.

After about six months of the rabbi's classes, some of my schoolmates started to become religious. I was shocked. These were sophisticated, thinking friends of mine. They weren't the type to run off to a cult and let themselves be brainwashed. But brainwashed they had been, and I felt that I had to take it upon myself to do something about it.

We started having meetings every Tuesday night at which I and another friend met with around four of the "converted" to argue and debate God's existence. I had no interest in the discussion itself; indeed the very topic was distasteful to me. But I felt a responsibility to save my mates from their newfound and eagerly embraced insanity.

We would often talk late into the night, with them eager to suck me in and me eager to suck them out. As you can imagine with so much suction going on, we didn't get all that far.

Life went on and I moved into Lark Lane. My old friends were becoming decidedly Orthodox and I was involved in a rather different lifestyle, which suited me much better. I liked my life and my season ticket to the Saturday soccer games where my team, Liverpool, were the kings of Europe. By April of my senior year, I had already been offered a scholarship to study aeronautical engineering at Caltech in California. That left me five months to coast.

I've met people much further away from Judaism than I was then, but I must say that at this time, I wasn't all that close.

So what happened next was quite a bombshell.

It was April, 1984. A few weeks earlier, the rabbi had invited me for his *Pesach seder* and I had accepted the invitation with the idea of canceling closer to the time. However, the rabbi didn't let me do that. On the day of the *seder*, one of his 'converts' called me to ask me for a lift. My car had broken down the day before, but where were we going? To a pub? To town? "To the rabbi's *Pesach seder*," was his shocking response. I stuttered and stammered and made excuses, but my fate was sealed. They were expecting me. They had cooked for me. They had set a place for me at the table. They were looking forward to having me. How could I not go?

Any thoughts of making an early getaway were shattered by the time we finally started at 10:00 p.m. I buckled down for the duration.

I'd been to family *seders* in the past and they were always the same. Who cares what Rabbi Eliezer said? What difference does it make if there were fifty or five hundred plagues? And my uncle's personal favorite: We are the ones who are free, so why do we have to eat matzah? Let the Egyptians eat this stuff! The only bit I ever looked forward to was when my two brothers-in-law got drunk on the four cups and danced on the table to the tune of *Chad Gadya*.

So I came that night expecting the usual bore. But boy was I surprised!

The rabbi brought the *seder* to life for me for the first time ever. Passover is not about what happened three thousand years ago. It's about who you are today. Personal freedom is something we are all striving for. Is a smoker free? A drug addict? Isn't slavery a very personal experience — and emancipation a potential that lies within us all? These were the type of questions the rabbi posed and answered throughout the *Haggadah*. Rabbi Eliezer was no longer talking about Egypt, he was talking about me. It was such a radical turnaround that it was mind-blowing. We chatted and argued and debated till four in the morning — and I was ready for more. I was loving every moment of it. Finally, I had found that Judaism actually spoke to me.

The rabbi suggested I stay the night. It was an innocuous enough suggestion, but it burst my bubble. Staying the night meant Synagogue the next morning. Then probably lunch, then another *seder*. Before I knew it, I'd be his latest success story. I envisioned a picture of myself pinned on his wall with 'convert of the month' emblazoned across the top. No way.

However, I had about a five-mile walk home. And the only real way was through a park called Sefton Park. I haven't been there in a while, and apparently they've made it into a nice place nowadays. But in 1984, it was not a place you walked through alone at four o'clock in the morning.

I had a very stark choice. Walk through the park — and risk my body. Stay at the rabbi's — and risk my soul. It was a no-brainer. I apologized profusely, explained that I had promised to call my parents the next day, and got out the door as quickly as possible.

The entrance to Sefton Park looked dark and foreboding. I picked up a stick and thought about everything that Ray had taught me. If someone attacked me, they could do almost anything to me and I would still be okay. The walk was terrifying but uneventful. I arrived at the other side safe and sound.

But then a thought hit me that stopped me in my tracks. So obvious and shocking was it that I couldn't continue walking for quite a few minutes.

What was wrong with me? Why was I so afraid? All the rabbi had ever offered me was honesty and truth. He had only said that he would present evidence and allow me to judge for myself. Why on earth was I running away? So terrified, in fact, that I would risk physical injury rather than investigate further. Lucidity flowed. I had confidence in my mind — if he could 'prove' to me that God existed, it meant God did. And what was the point in hiding from it? Surely it was better to face the consequences sooner rather than later. And if he could not prove it to me, then I could happily carry on with wherever life took me. It was a win-win situation.

The more I thought about it over the next few days, the more sense it made. I saw the rabbi and my friends with a different attitude. I was open. I was ready to hear the evidence. And hear it I did. It took me a year and a half to be ready to listen, but only a couple of weeks to feel compelled by what I heard.

I was planning to take a year off university and spend the winter in Austria, getting a license to be a ski instructor. But I had nothing to do for the summer. Most of my friends were going to *yeshivah* in Jerusalem for six weeks. I felt that before I went to Southern California and likely severed my already tenuous connection to my Jewish heritage, I owed it to myself to do a proper investigation. I had nothing else scheduled. I was impressed by the evidence I had heard. What else was there to do but go to *yeshivah* with my friends?

Those six weeks turned into seven years. I never got my ski instructor license — in fact, I went from skiing twice a year for fifteen years to not skiing at all for the next fifteen years. But I have to say that when I finally did get on skis again (on a honeymoon with my present wife, Chana), it was just like riding a bicycle. You never forget.

I gave up my scholarship at Caltech. Instead, I studied long and hard hours at Aish HaTorah *Yeshiva*, learned to teach, became a rabbi, and married Elana. I remember saying in my wedding speech that the road to Judaism had been a long one — at times difficult and even discouraging. But had I known from the outset that this was the road one takes to find a girl like Elana, that and that alone would have made it all worthwhile...

A Match Made in Heaven?

T he first time I met Elana, she was eighteen and I was twenty-two. We were both working as *madrichim* for Aish HaTorah, a Jewish outreach organization, on a program called Discovery, in the Old City of Jerusalem. It was a match made in heaven — sort of.

As I was waiting in the lobby of the Discovery Centre one morning, I glanced over and saw a young lady enter the room. She was dressed like a schoolgirl and seemed even younger. Why was she here? She looked religious, so she couldn't be a participant in the program. And surely Moshe, the program director, could not have hired her as a *madrichah*? How could this Orthodox little girl relate to the secular worldly people in their twenties and thirties who would be passing through our doors?

I immediately went to clear up the matter with Moshe. "Yes, she is a *madrichah*," he told me.

"Well, then, fire her!" I shot back. "We are a professional organization, trying to reach young Jews who don't relate to Judaism. This girl just doesn't have what it takes." But my appeals, fortuitously, did not make a dent.

How could I possibly imagine that only twelve years later, I would sit with her in a house in London as she breathed her last breaths and returned her holy soul to God?

Elana didn't see me that day, but two days later we had a *kumzitz*, a gathering around a bonfire. Someone brought a guitar and everyone sang along. She looked over at me and noticed me for the first time. As she told me later, her thoughts were not wildly different from mine. "He can't be a participant because of the black *yarmulke* that he wears. But he's swigging beer out of a bottle and smoking a cigarette. How could Aish hire such a lowlife to be a counselor?!"

As I said, a match made in heaven...

We were assigned to work on the same program, so eventually we had to speak to one another. And when we did, I was surprised to find that I actually enjoyed the conversation. As the days and weeks of summer progressed, I found myself talking to Elana more and more. Discovery was an Orthodox program and counselors did not socialize, but somehow, we managed to find excuses to talk about issues that were, of course, absolutely crucial to the running of the program.

I started to find myself really liking Elana. But it just couldn't be. She was right out of high school — so naive. She wasn't classical 'rebbetzin material' — and I was soon going to be a rabbi. But the more I tried to avoid her, the more we seemed to meet. I was surprised at myself. She was taller than me. (But so are most people!) She was quiet and soft spoken — so unlike myself. She was one of those sweet and innocent *FFB's* (religious from birth) that we *BT's* (newly religious) didn't even think about; and she was such a goodie-goodie — and how I hated goodie-goodies! I couldn't figure out what I liked about her, but we managed to talk for hours on end without running out of things to say.

I wasn't marriage-minded at the time, so I didn't think of her as someone whom I might date. But I did have a friend, Avi, who had been unsuccessfully dating for quite a while. As time went on and I thought more and more about Elana, it occurred to me that it might be a good idea to set them up. Still, I didn't want to set my friend up with a girl I'd just had a few conversations with, so I started making inquiries — as is usual in the Orthodox world. The more people I asked, the more I was impressed. I didn't hear anything negative from anyone, only amazing praise. She was just too good to be true. I said to myself, *I know I'm a good friend, but why am I setting Avi up with her? Even though I'm not quite ready to date, shouldn't I go out with her myself?*

I asked Rabbi Appel, the senior rabbi at Discovery, if he would find out whether or not she was dating. He got on the case immediately and she told him she had not started dating yet, but who did he have in mind?

"Why are you asking if you're not dating yet?" he asked.

"Well, I'm not dating, but if it happens to be Shaul (or Stevie as I was known then), I might reconsider..."

Rabbi Appel came back to me to tell me we were going out Wednesday night. I put up a brave fight. I protested that I had only asked him to find out if she had started dating, not to organise a date! We argued back and forth, but in the end, I very reluctantly acquiesced.

Wednesday came and Elana acted as if nothing had changed. At the Discovery program that day, she didn't blink an eye. She didn't look at me, she didn't smile, she didn't even glance in my direction. I figured Rabbi Appel must be pulling a fast one on me. Was I really going out with her that evening?

Finally, the day was almost over. I couldn't wait any longer. She went into the counselors' room and I followed. I found her looking for something in a cupboard. Sensing my presence, she slowly closed the cupboard doors, looked me straight in the eye, and smiled at me for the first time — a smile that would be her hallmark for as long as I knew her, even during her darkest hours; a smile of such goodness, such sweetness that I knew right there and then that if I were lucky enough to marry her, I would be truly blessed. "I'll be ready in ten minutes," she said, still smiling, as she walked out of the room.

After the first date, neither of us had any doubts. We got along so well! We had similar goals, similar values, similar dreams — similar everything. And we had such fun together. We were like teenagers who couldn't stop giggling the whole night. I guess, to be fair, Elana actually was a teenager.

We went out six times in seven days because Elana was returning to America after that. At the end of our last date, we knew it was too early to get officially engaged, but each of us also knew that it was going to happen. Three months later, after finishing my rabbinic degree, I went to America and we got engaged. The only way we could describe the whole process — and we quoted it again and again and again — was a verse from Psalms 13:6: "I will sing to God for He has bestowed His goodness upon me." It was all so right and so perfect. It seemed to us that stories like this only happened in fairy tales, not in real life. We kept pinching ourselves to make sure that we were not dreaming.

Elana finished her year at university and I came to America for the wedding. The *chuppah* part of our wedding video focuses on me taking tissue after tissue from my father to wipe away my tears of joy. I was so happy. I was marrying, not the girl of my boyhood dreams, but the girl with whom I could create new and more mature dreams — a *bas Yisrael* in the deepest sense of the word.

Every day, I wake up in the morning and thank God for Elana. She was a wonderful dream — all too fleeting a dream — but a wonderful dream nevertheless.

I will not bore you with the details of our life from our wedding in 1990 until *Rosh HaShanah* 1998. We set up home in Jerusalem, then moved to England to set up Aish HaTorah UK. We had four beautiful children — each of whom reminds me of Elana in his or her own special way. We had our ups and downs, as all marriages do, but generally we found more happiness in our relationship than we had ever imagined existed.

The summer of 1998 was a particularly difficult one for us. We had our last two children quite close to each other and so we had two babies in the house. I remember our whole family going to America in August. Neither of the babies had a seat, so Elana and I sat on opposite sides of the aisle. As the flight was beginning its descent, one of the babies threw up over the armrest. The other baby, on the opposite side, took one look and threw up also. The plane was going down, so the vomit started rolling down the aisle. Everyone had their seatbelts fastened, including the stewardesses, so all we could do was sit there and watch. Needless to say, we were not the most popular people on the flight!

Having two babies at the same time started to become overwhelming for us. We started to feel challenged by our circumstances — perhaps a little frustrated even. Life was not going the way we wanted it to.

But all that was nothing compared to what was to come next.

Elana first felt the lump right before our trip. She was twenty-seven years old and nursing a baby. It couldn't be serious. People don't get cancer at this age. But they do.

We went to the doctor as soon as we returned from America, and he said it was surely just an infected milk duct. "Come back in two weeks if it hasn't gone away." And come back we did…a few days before *Rosh HaShanah*. The lump had not gone away; it had grown bigger — quite a bit bigger. And now she had a lump in her neck, as well. The doctor was still sure it was an infection, but he sent us to see a surgeon just to put our mind at rest for the holidays. We went right after *Rosh HaShanah*. The surgeon was very nice. He asked for the details and gave us one small bit of reassurance — reassurance that later on we certainly could have done without. He told us that it could not be cancer because cancer could not possibly grow as fast as this lump had.

But he said he would do a mammogram just in case.

The doctor in charge of the mammogram did an ultrasound first. She said that she did not know what it was, but it did not look like cancer. She was about to send us home when I suggested the mammogram that we had been sent for in the first place.

"Why not?" She said. "It can't do any harm!"

It was during the mammogram that we started to worry seriously. Once the doctor had started looking, she wanted to look at another angle and another and another. She kept us in the X-ray room for almost an hour. Then she disappeared. I searched and discovered her hiding place, wanting to make sure she still thought it wasn't cancer. Suddenly she turned very professional on me. She could not give me results; I had to refer to our surgeon. But could she at least put our minds at rest before the weekend, I asked.

She would send her results to the surgeon and we would see him on Monday. And that was that.

The next couple of days were tense. It was a painful weekend and we were both on edge.

We got to the surgeon's office early in the morning and he kept us waiting for over an hour and a half. He seemed to be looking for an excuse not to see us. Finally, very reluctantly, he called us into his office. We already pretty much knew what he had in store for us.

"It's malignant," was all he said.

But we refused to understand.

"Are you sure? Could it be a mistake? Is there any other possibility?"

We were desperate to cling to any straw.

But there were to be no straws.

Elana had primary breast cancer, with secondaries in her lymph nodes and both lungs. Stage 4 and aggressive. Given the limitations of modern medicine at that time and still today, that was tantamount to a death sentence — a slow death sentence, perhaps, but a sure one, nonetheless.

For almost three years we battled together, grew together, lived our days together to their fullest until, in August of 2001, Elana passed away. That beautiful girl who had first smiled that wonderful smile at me all those years before; the girl who had given me four beautiful children; the girl who had never been sick — had always been so robust and healthy — until she got cancer; the girl who I had never, ever heard say a bad word about another human being; the wonderful *bas Yisrael* with whom I was so desperate to spend the rest of my life. Gone... Gone... Forever... She had left me a widower; left me with four young children, alone to face the world.

But Elana and I had been determined from the very outset that our experience of her illness would be a positive one — which it was. We grew a lot; we learned a lot and we came to our own understanding of the role of adversity in our lives. Subsequently, I came to my own understanding – alone this time – of loss and of learning to live life without those whom we have loved.

I have presented what I have learned in the hope that others will benefit from the lessons of our experiences.

Elana

I want to share a few stories about Elana. I'm not just indulging — I truly believe that others might find her as inspirational as I and many others did. During the *shivah*, so many people had said that they could only describe her as an angel. She was not an angel. As her husband, I knew that. But if anyone I know came close, it was certainly Elana.

During her last days, she was so sick. Cancer is an incredibly horrific disease; those who have been with a loved one in the final stages of cancer know what I mean. (And I pray for those who haven't that they should never have to.) She was as thin as a rake. She was in a great deal of pain. She could not keep much down in the way of food. But worst of all was her breathing. She felt constantly as though she was suffocating. And suffocating she was, with the cancer slowly filling up the space of both her lungs. Over and over again, I would ask her how she was doing. Over and over again — without any exception at all — she would smile her beautiful smile at me and say that she was doing great. It was not a show. She really was doing great.

One time, during Elana's final six weeks, one of the Jewish nurses responsible for her care walked over on *Shabbos* and spent a couple of hours checking things out. Finally, she said good-bye to Elana and began to leave. Elana suddenly panicked and didn't want her to go. At this point, it took her about ten minutes to catch enough breath to speak even a few words, but she motioned at me to come over. I was very anxious to hear what was distressing her so. Finally, gathering all her energy to speak, she was able to whisper in my ear. Amidst all her pain, Elana had noticed that it was raining outside and that the nurse did not have a proper coat. She insisted that the nurse take her own coat so she would not get wet on her way home.

Her concern for others even in the midst of her own tragedy was one of Elana's hallmarks.

During her final *Shabbos* in this world, we had guests over. They were discussing our china and I told them it was thirty years old. Elana immediately whispered to her sister to say that it is still made today. I was surprised that Elana should be concerned to point out that her china was not out of date until her sister explained to me that this was not her point. Elana had told her that she did not want the guests to be worried about breaking or chipping something that was irreplaceable.

I regularly felt humbled in her presence.

We knew from the outset that the cancer was in her lungs and so, having spent many a late night on the Internet, I realized that a cough was a very bad sign. During the three years of her illness, she would occasionally start coughing, and I would always be terrified until it went away. During her final months, she developed a cough that just wouldn't go away. I think that we both knew deep down that it wasn't going to.

She started to act rather strangely during this period and it was only later that I realized why. Very often, we would be in a room together and suddenly she would run out for a moment. Even mid conversation, she would say she had to step out quickly, and she would return a moment later. At the time it seemed strange. But as the weeks went on, I understood that she was leaving the room to cough, because she knew how much it scared me to hear it. The trouble she went to so that I wouldn't hear her cough was quite unbelievable.

In the end, she could no longer keep up the pretense, and I realized that her cough had become so much worse than I thought. She had been doing a very good job thinking of me and concealing her pain. Most people, I believe, would have wanted their spouse's sympathy and support (I know that I would have) but Elana was willing to bear her own pain privately and alone in order to spare me from mine.

As I said, I don't remember ever hearing a bad word from her mouth about another person. A childhood friend of Elana attended the *shivah*, the seven day mourning period, from America. He said the same. He never heard a bad word about anyone from her. Even when she knew something about someone that I wanted to know, she would refuse to tell me and was extremely careful not to hint at anything, either. If I began to guess, she would go so far as to make up stories to mislead me. If I was trying to get something out of her, she would just refuse to talk to me, in case she carelessly gave something away that might be detrimental about someone else. In general, she was a very easygoing person, but when she wanted to be stubborn about this, she was very stubborn indeed!

When she left for America after we had been going out for our first week, she forgot her diary in my apartment. Here was my opportunity to see what she really felt about me; to see what was really going on in her mind. I knew I shouldn't, but it was such a temptation that I could not resist. I found it full of sincere love. Later that day, there was a message from her on my answer machine. She was desperate to get a hold of me before she left, to tell me about the diary. She wasn't worried to get her diary back. She simply said she knew that I would be unable to resist reading it and that before I did, she wanted to tell me that I could, so that I would do so with her permission as opposed to without.

Another example of her full consideration for others was when she was in labor. She was clearly in tremendous pain during each contraction. She wanted a natural labor, so she took no form of pain relief. Even during a contraction when she was virtually holding back from screaming, she would look over at me and say she wasn't really in pain, and that it just looked like it. She said that she knew it hurt me more to see her in pain than it did for her to be in pain and I should not worry because things were not what they seemed to be. (I said to her that for sure I must be in more pain than she was, but not to worry, she could make it up to me after the birth!)

Seriously, though, she had no concern for herself — even at a time when she had every right to. She was only concerned about me. It wasn't about her pain, it was about my pain at seeing her in pain. That's all she worried about. To her, seeing someone else in pain was infinitely worse than feeling her own pain and she assumed that everyone else felt the same way. Selflessness was so completely natural to her that she could not imagine someone relating to the world differently.

Our second child, Shifra, was born on *seder* night, the first night of Passover. Elana insisted on doing the *Haggadah*, the ritual retelling of the story of leaving Egypt, in the delivery room in between contractions. She would calm down from the contraction and say, "Okay, let's drink the second cup of wine now" or "Let's eat the matzah" or "Quickly, let's read some more of the story before the next one comes." We made it as far as the *afikoman*, almost the end, before she gave birth and only then did she decide that now her priority lay with her newborn baby, not the *seder*.

During the difficult years of Elana's illness, we had a young, Romanian cleaning lady help out in the house a couple of times a week. Her name was Michaela.

On numerous occasions, I came home and found Michaela and Elana deep in conversation. Sometimes Michaela had tears in her eyes. When I asked Elana what was going on, she would tell me that she was advising Michaela on her relationship with her boyfriend or her parents or the difficulties she was encountering getting permission to remain in England.

If I asked for more details, Elana would always decline. Michaela had confided in her privately, and I knew there was no point in even trying to get it out of her. In Elana's *shivah* book, Michaela wrote that she looked up to Elana as a mother.

No one was beneath her; no one was unworthy of her attention. If there was another human being in need — even a cleaning lady whom she was paying to work, not to chat — she would drop everything and be there.

Finally, when eulogizing her on the thirtieth day of her passing, Rabbi Noah Weinberg said that it's not everyone who can do a kindness at their own funeral. Let me explain.

Her funeral was on August 9, 2001. Israelis might recognize the date. The funeral was due to be held at 10 a.m. in Jerusalem, but for some reason, our flight from London was delayed by two hours. There was a strange electrical fault on the plane, and they took everyone off the plane and told us the flight was canceled and the next flight would be in twelve hours. Then they suddenly found the solution and told everyone to board the plane. Some passengers had already taken buses to a hotel for the night, but the airline personnel brought them back.

Since the flight was delayed two hours, so was the funeral. Instead of being held at 10 a.m., it was called for 12:00 that afternoon and lasted until around 2 p.m. Two of our students from Aish in England had planned to go to the funeral at 10 a.m. and then have lunch at a restaurant called Sbarro's in Jerusalem. They planned to meet at the restaurant at 1:30 p.m. Due to the delay of the funeral, their lunch meeting was canceled. That afternoon, at around 2 p.m., a suicide bomber walked into Sbarro's and blew himself up, killing fifteen innocent people. Had the funeral not been delayed, these two students would likely have been among the victims. I'm no *Kabbalist*, and I'm not usually into mystical things, but I certainly feel that Elana had a hand in this.

(You may ask at this point — as probably you should — yes, but what about the people who did die in the bombing? Didn't God look after them, as well? Why wasn't the funeral they were going to delayed also? This type of question is, of course, the whole purpose of this book and I hope that I have provided some level of satisfying answers.)

A few months after Elana's passing, someone who knew her told me that he had spoken to a *Kabbalist* about her. As I said, I'm not so into *Kabbalists* myself, but what he said was interesting. He said that he knew Elana's soul, even though he had never met her. He said that he had never said this about anyone else before, but he saw her soul resting with the matriarchs (Sarah, Rivkah, Rachel, and Leah) in the World to Come. Had he said it about almost anyone else, I would probably have laughed. But about Elana — I didn't need to be a *Kabbalist* to know that he was right.

These few pages cannot truly do justice to the thirty years of life of a very special young woman. I hope that you have at least gained a sense of who Elana was and why she had such a massive impact on all who were fortunate enough to know her. May her soul be bound in the bonds of eternal life.

In Elana's Words

Elana Rosenblatt passed away in London on August 8, 2001. In her thirty short years, she accomplished more than many do in twice or three times that amount of time. Always smiling, always giving, always thinking about others — never about herself. Even in her final illness, when she was weak and in great distress, she was always positive, confident in God's love for her, whatever may be. This article is based on classes she gave about a year before she passed away.

Isn't Life Beautiful?
By Elana Rosenblatt

When I first felt the lump, I was sure that it had everything to do with nursing my six-month-old baby, and nothing at all to do with cancer. I live in England and I was soon going to America to see my parents, so I pushed it to the back of my mind. When I returned home, I could tell the lump had gotten bigger. It was time to see the doctor.

"Don't worry," he said. "Come back in two weeks — if it's still there."

It was still there. And it was close to Rosh HaShanah. The doctor said, "I'm sure it's nothing, but I want you to have a clear mind for the holidays, so I'm sending you to a surgeon for an evaluation."

I went to the surgeon, who sent me for a mammogram and a biopsy — again, just to be sure it was nothing. Nobody wanted to believe that a twenty-seven-year-old new mother could have breast cancer.

A few days before Yom Kippur we returned to the surgeon. We sat in his waiting room for what seemed like an eternity. Finally, we were called in.

He looked at me and said, "It's cancer." It was like a fist in my gut.

Yet life continued. That day it was my turn to do carpool, so my husband and I went straight from the surgeon's office to my daughter's school. We were quite late, and my carpool kids were all waiting in the headmistress's room.

As I went in, I figured the headmistress was going to have to know sooner or later; I might as well tell her now. When she heard my news, I saw such love and care in her eyes. She said, "Anything you need, we're here for you." She was someone I hardly knew, as it was my daughter's first year in the school, but the love that I felt from her was absolute. This was my first taste of so many loving acts to follow from friends and strangers alike.

We got home, and I dropped the kids off at unsuspecting neighbors. Now my husband and I had a chance to talk.

It was a very emotional time, and we both had a lot we needed to say, but there was one idea that repeatedly came up: God does not do anything that is not perfect.

Life is a puzzle. As we add the pieces of the puzzle one by one, the picture becomes clearer. Sometimes we're not sure where to put a piece; we can't even imagine how it's going to fit. We hold it up and turn it over in our hand and we feel sure that someone must have made a mistake — surely this piece does not belong to this puzzle.

There is no mistake. This piece belongs. As we put together this jigsaw puzzle of our lives, the pieces fit together so beautifully that the seams between them seem to disappear and an awesome picture emerges.

Two hours before I lit Yom Kippur candles, we got a phone call. At first the doctor had been only 99 percent sure the cancer was metastatic. Now she was 100 percent sure.

I was able to see this call as a blessing, too. After all, I had found this out before Yom Kippur and still had the opportunity of this holy day before me. This is the day God is closest to us, the day on which we have the most special relationship with Him. I felt that my fate was not yet sealed.

Sukkos came four days later. We left our sturdy home and went out to live in a flimsy sukkah. The sukkah, with its rickety walls and roof of branches that doesn't protect us from the elements, teaches us that our protection comes from Heaven, not from anything in the physical world. With these thoughts in mind, I started chemotherapy.

As time went on, the jigsaw was making more and more sense. But there are always pieces that don't fit straight away.

Nietzsche said that man can deal with any "what" as long as he has a good enough "why." Let's say you're working out to get in shape. Your muscles are killing you. You're stretching to the breaking point. But you persevere — because it means enough to you. It's painful, but it's worth it. The "why" overcomes the "what."

This is pain that you choose. What about when the pain comes from outside of you? Picture a runner training for the Olympics. The trainer has him running thirty miles a day. He also has to be up very early, keep to a very strict diet, and lift weights for hours. You look at this and think, *Why is the trainer putting him through so much torture?* But the trainer's not putting him through torture; the trainer knows he has the potential to win. And he wants to bring that potential into reality.

When I go for chemotherapy and it takes them six tries to find a vein, not one of those times was unnecessary. Each jab was exactly perfect for what I need. There are no accidents.

Worry, not pain, is my enemy.

There are two things I do to strengthen myself:

First, I make a list of worries that never came true — all the things I worried over that never actually materialized, leaving me with only the hours I had wasted.

Second, several times a day I go over different aspects of the special relationship I have with God. I do this to stay one step ahead of the doubt. And one step ahead of the fear.

Prayer is part of this relationship. Will my prayers be answered the way I want them answered? This I can't know. But I believe that if I ask for God's help, the outcome is more likely to be something easier to accept as beautiful than something harder to accept as beautiful.

Thankfully, I've been feeling well. Cancer is a very funny disease. You can have a cold and not be able to get out of bed, and you can have cancer and do just about everything.

But cancer is also very serious, and sometimes "Mommy's not feeling well." The way I look at it, though, I'm really no different from anyone else. No one knows what's around the corner. We all pray that it should be something good and easily recognizable as beautiful. But who knows what tomorrow will bring?

That's how I deal with the children. I haven't said to them, "Cancer can be fatal," although there are people on the block that have died from cancer and they know it. They have me around today and I'm thankful I can be a mother to them.

Tomorrow is another story — and it would be, even if I didn't have cancer.

My children are eight, six, almost four, and two. It's not easy. In fact, it's incredibly difficult. There have been moments of anger. I've never been able to come out and say, "Thank You, God, for giving me cancer." That's a tough one. I've tried to be very, very real with my anger and not to push it back down. I've tried to really face it head-on.

And I've found that when I accept the anger, it becomes less of an enemy. The same with the fear. Sometimes I have to say, "Okay, I'm scared." But I'm not going to let that fear get the better of me.

I wasn't like this three years ago. I'm two generations from the Holocaust. My grandparents lost almost their entire families. For many years I was angry with God. My relationship was not one of love; it was one of fear. My kids would say, "Mommy, when I'm ten...," and I would think, *God willing, you should live to be ten*. I wasn't the most positive person. I wouldn't say those words, but I would certainly think them.

I've grown since then. When I thank God for the little things, it helps me know that He is with me for the big things. I thank Him for my food and my arms and my legs, and when I go to the hospital, though it's the last place in the world I want to be, I thank Him for that, too. I know He's there with me.

I try to take pleasure in the good instead of focusing on the bad. When I walk in for chemotherapy and the nurse smiles at me, I try to take pleasure in that. She could greet me with a scowl on her face and make the whole experience a lot worse.

Life is like a train ride. The nice thing about this train ride is that everyone has first-class tickets. But we often see people, even ourselves, riding third class. Why is that? Circumstance is never the problem. It's what we conjure up in our imagination that really hurts us. Often the physical pain and the emotional anguish are relatively easy to deal with, but we torment ourselves with worry and fear. Herein lies my challenge. Cancer is not a third-class ticket. Cancer is a guidebook to what first-class has to offer.

Life is beautiful. Let's make it eternally beautiful. And really enjoy.

Part Three

Remarriage

Really, this book should have concluded at the end of the previous chapter, but I felt that it would be of value to include details of my remarriage in order to show that life really does go on. I also hope that it will provide benefit to those experiencing similar difficulties; and finally, it gives me the opportunity to honor my remarkable wife Chana, who has made my life brighter than I could have ever dreamed possible.

Marrying a second time is always difficult. Marrying after going through the intense relationship that I went through with Elana during her last few weeks was surely impossible.

At the same time, I knew that I still had so much to give to a marriage — if anything I felt I had more to give after what I had been through. And I knew also that our children desperately needed a mother.

There are so many challenges that one faces in a situation like this — not least of all a new wife trying to fill the shoes of someone who was so respected, so loved, and so cherished.

I know of cases in which a second wife comes into a situation like this with incredibly good intentions and is undermined by family and friends and anyone who felt close to the first wife. A misguided sense of loyalty seems to make people feel that they must defend the position of the first wife from an opportunist impostor. For us too, not everyone found themselves able to support Chana in her new role. Chana did not judge them because she understood how difficult it must be for them. She simply reached out to them and was successful to a greater or lesser extent. At the same time, the support Chana received from so many other family members and friends, was quite incredible. And those who were there for her at the outset, are those with whom she retains cherished relationships today.

I know that it doesn't always work this way, but Chana had an amazing realization at a certain point – that for those who judged her and gave her a hard time, it was nothing personal. It was not Chana Rosenblatt they were upset with. It could have been Rivkah Rosenblatt, Sara Rosenblatt or Esther Rosenblatt and it would not have mattered. In their own minds, because of their own pain, they simply could not accept another woman taking on Elana's role as my wife and our children's mother. Seeing and understanding that made it so much easier for Chana. Rather than be upset, she felt compassion for their pain.

Every day, without exception, I thank God for Elana. And every day, without exception, I also thank God for Chana. I feel doubly blessed to have been given two such special women with whom to share different periods of my life.

While the process leading up to my marrying Elana felt almost akin to a fairy tale, the process leading up to marrying Chana was rockier, more painful, and more real — but no less special in its own way.

Chana came to help with our children eight months before Elana passed away. At the time, she was eighteen years old. She is number six of twelve children and was very used to taking responsibility for kids. As far as she was concerned, she was coming for a short time to help a family whose mother was sick. She thought she would stay a little while, the mother would get better, and she would leave. She wasn't at all prepared for what was about to happen to her.

As Chana was a young woman in my house, I steered very clear of her, but her relationship with Elana blossomed. During those eight months, Chana and Elana became the best of friends, in spite of their age difference. Elana trusted Chana implicitly with the children and shared with her many of her values and dreams in child rearing. Chana learned from Elana, grew from Elana, and came to love Elana very deeply. In the short period of time that they knew each other, they developed a very special relationship. When she was really not well, Chana was the one that Elana called in to ask how I was doing and to make sure I had what I needed. She wanted to set Chana up with her brother, but as usual, God had other and always better plans.

After Elana passed away, Chana was the woman the children initially turned to for their emotional needs. But I didn't think it was right of me to place such a burden on an eighteen-year-old girl. I asked her if she wanted to leave, even encouraged her to do so, but she didn't feel that she could abandon the children when they needed her. She was a young woman with so many opportunities, but for her the children, even though they were not her own, came first. To be sure, there were those who questioned her motives — as is to be expected in a situation like this — but time and events would prove just how sincere she was.

A few months after Elana passed away, I started to think about getting married again. It was soon, but I had four young children and I knew that I could not give them all that they needed. I thought about Chana, about her relationship with the kids and with Elana. I remember taking a walk with my eldest daughter, who was eight at the time, and discussing the concept of my getting married again. She had a picture of a 'wicked stepmother' and was terrified at the thought. I asked her if there was anyone whom she would be happy with. I went through a list of people she knew and felt close to and each one got a very clear no. I saved Chana for last and asked her what she thought. "Yes, Abba. Please marry Chana," was her immediate answer. (She has since told me that she would never have said that if she knew Chana would cut back on the candies once we married!)

It was a painful decision for me, but after much thought I decided that Chana was too young. There was a sixteen year age difference between us. She deserved a young man with no baggage — someone who would cherish her and be excited by her without another woman in the back of his mind. I felt it was selfish and unfair of me even to consider her. Even if she was interested, I believed it was only because she was caught up in the emotions of the situation. I was convinced that if she married me, she would regret doing so at a later date.

Despite the fact that Elana's sister had stayed on to give the children support, we were a single man and single woman caring for the same children in the same house, and it was not a healthy situation. I knew that the only fair and sensible course of action was for me to insist that she leave. It was painful for me, painful for her, and even more painful for the kids, but in the long run, I honestly believed I was making the right decision for the family.

And so, one year after her arrival and four months after Elana's passing, Chana left for America.

We missed her. But I knew we would get over it. I decided to buckle down to some serious dating.

Given how my relationship had developed with Elana, dating wasn't really something I had done before. I found myself coming home and crying for hours after a date. How could I marry someone who was not Elana? I felt so confused and lost with the whole process. Should I look for someone in the same circumstances as myself? But that would mean double the baggage. I'd heard of marriages that fell apart because the children didn't get along with each other. Or should I look for someone who had never married before? But how would they even begin to relate to what I had been through?

I told myself that at the very least, I needed someone totally different from Elana. I wanted someone who excelled in areas that Elana hadn't. That was the only way I might save myself from constant comparisons. Other than that, I had no idea what I was looking for. Nothing that wasn't Elana made sense to me.

Dating was an incredibly distressing and challenging experience. However, I knew that things would get better. I knew that the pain would pass and I would again experience incredible goodness in my life. I knew that *Hashem* had wonderful plans and that this was a piece of the jigsaw puzzle and one day I would see how perfectly it fitted. But it's one thing to know these things and another to be able actually to live with them. During Elana's final illness, I had had Elana there to help me focus properly. Now I was on my own and I wasn't coping well.

I went through a number of difficult experiences, including, unfortunately, a broken engagement; but in the end, I just couldn't hide from the way I felt about Chana. She had supported me and our children in our hour of greatest need. She cared deeply about my family. She loved Elana. I knew that she had an understanding of what marrying a man in my situation would mean for her and the sacrifices she would have to make — and I was confident that she was ready and willing to make those sacrifices. I had felt that I knew what was best. I had thought that I had it all worked out. And for six months I had suffered the consequences. In the end, I came to the realization that God knew best. And He was simply offering Chana and I the gift of our relationship. As always, with God, a free gift given with love. And, finally, I found myself able to let go of my own personal thinking and embrace it.

As had happened with Elana, it didn't take all that long. After a few conversations on the phone, we both knew it was right and we would be getting married. Everything seemed to fall into place. It seemed clear once again just how perfectly God was running His world. The jigsaw pieces were starting to make so much more sense.

I didn't want to get engaged over the phone, so Chana came to England for a day. For the first time in a long time, I felt a sense of hope. The fog was starting to clear for me. As with Elana, when I proposed and when Chana said yes, my world seemed to take on a whole new level of color and excitement. (Although I did get a bit of culture shock when I got down on one knee to propose and my Israeli, soon to be fiancée, said to me that she would not say 'yes' until I stood up again and stopped being so ridiculous!)

When I told the kids, they were excited, but in light of my broken engagement a little skeptical. "Are you really going to do it this time, *Abba*?" was their response. "We'll believe it when we see it."

As the wedding drew near, the kids and I were so excited. But the night before, there was still one issue to deal with. What would the kids call Chana? Of course, they all knew her extremely well by the name Chana. But once we were married, this just wouldn't be right. "*Ima*" was the name they had called Elana and was clearly not appropriate. "Mum" was completely alien to Chana, since she had been brought up in Israel. We were all a bit stuck. I sat with the four kids on the floor of our hotel room in Jerusalem and we discussed ideas. Auntie Chana — doesn't quite fit. *Ima* — no good. Mummy — no way!! The kids came up with quite a few funnies. We considered "Wicked Stepmother" for a while, but it was rejected because it was a bit too long. We thought maybe just "Wicked" for short, but we weren't sure that Chana would like it. "Step" or "Steppy" were rejected by me, even though the kids liked them the best.

After almost an hour, when we were starting to despair, Shifra, my eldest daughter, hit upon the perfect name. "How about 'Mima'?" she said. It wasn't Mum, but it wasn't *Ima* either. It was a composite that gave the sense of Chana being Ima without explicitly stating it. The moment Shifra said it, we all knew it was right. There was really no discussion about it because we all knew just how perfect it was. Elana will always be *Ima* for them and have a very special place in their hearts. But their new Mima would be Chana and she would be the one to give them the love they needed from here on in.

I had always wanted a Jerusalem wedding and was disappointed when Elana and I got married in America. It wasn't the way I would have chosen for it to happen, but now God granted me my wish.

I cry at most weddings, but in Jerusalem, I cry at every wedding. When I hear the words, *"Od yishama b'arei Yehudah u'vechutzos Yerushalayim* — Once again will be heard in the hills of Judah and the courtyards of Jerusalem, the sound of joy and the sound of happiness, the sound of a groom and the sound of a bride,"* (Jeremiah 33:10-11) I always feel a swelling of emotion. I visualize the prophet Jeremiah standing on a hillside looking down as the Jews leave Israel in chains for Babylon. I imagine him with tears streaming down his face. He would be justified to feel deep despair, but instead he prophesies a prophecy of hope — a prophecy that once again there will be happiness in Jerusalem, there will be weddings and celebrations. I think of Jeremiah and then I think of the wedding I am at. Here I am in direct fulfillment of his 2,500-year-old prophecy. I am standing in Jerusalem witnessing a wedding — exactly as he had said Jews would. How fortunate is our generation to see it come true, to see his dream fulfilled. Jeremiah, all those years ago, was prophesying about me... Like I say, I cannot help but cry.

And now it would be my own wedding.

On the day of the wedding I visited Elana's grave on *Har HaMenuchos* cemetery. I knew that she would approve. I knew how she felt about Chana and I knew that she would want me to be happy and the children to have a mother who loved them. It was a bittersweet experience for me, but I felt at one with her.

For me, the wedding was about me and Chana. But for my kind hearted Chana this wedding was not just for me and her. It was also for 'our' children. She made an incredible effort to be sure that they had new clothes for the wedding, that the girls had their hair done in a fancy style, that they were taken care of and looked after at every point. She found friends to care for them before, during, and after the wedding. While I would have been happy to forget about them for the week of *sheva berachos* and focus on our relationship instead, Chana insisted that we be in touch regularly. So many people remarked to me how beautiful it was to see Chana dancing with my daughters and sitting with them on her lap in the bridal chair.

She was a twenty-year-old bride. This was her special day. But her concern lay with making sure that my children — that our children — were happy. It was a truly special occasion that one had to witness to fully appreciate.

Once again, our wedding video shows me taking tissue after tissue as I cry under the *chuppah*. Yes, I cried at the thought that now I was not just watching, but actually taking part in the fulfillment of Jeremiah's ancient prophecy. But I also cried in deep happiness and gratitude — exactly as I had the first time around. I was marrying a very special *bas Yisrael*; a girl who was ready to risk marrying someone who still loved someone else; a girl who more than anything wanted to give our children a stable, warm, and loving home; a girl whom I felt would never replace Elana, but who would feel as strongly about me as Elana had and whom I could feel as strongly about as I had about Elana. A girl who Elana had loved and had been loved by Elana, too. I felt that *Hashem* had found the perfect situation for me and I was overwhelmed by His kindness. I was looking forward to our marriage with great hope. As I write the third edition of this book, thirteen years (and four more children) later, all of those hopes have been fulfilled. With compound interest.

I spoke to someone about marrying again not long after Elana died. He had been through what I had been through ten years earlier and had remarried a year after his wife passed away. I asked if he had found the same happiness in his second marriage as he had in his first. Not the same, he had responded. Different, but equal.

That is how I feel about Chana. She is not Elana. But I don't need her to be Elana. I need her to be Chana. And as Chana, I appreciate her for who she is in the way that I appreciated Elana for who she was. There is no comparison. I don't believe I felt more strongly about either. Just differently. And in a very different way I am as happy with Chana as I was with Elana.

In bringing up the children, Chana is a student of Elana. Like I said, Elana taught Chana an incredible amount about being a mother and Chana always feels that she wants to bring up the children the way that Elana would have. She remembers Elana well, thinks of her often, talks to the children regularly about her, and feels no sense of insecurity about her.

When Chana came into the house, I made sure all the pictures of Elana had been taken down and put away. Gradually, one by one, Chana put them back. She wants our children to cherish the memory of their *Ima* and knows that pictures play an important role.

Never once, even in times of frustration, have I heard Chana refer to any of the kids as "your children." They are always "our children." We have since been blessed with four more children and Chana relates to them no differently than to the first four. For her, she has eight children who are all equal in her eyes.

At Akiva, our eldest son's, wedding, two years ago Chana walked Akiva's bride down the aisle, as is customary at an Orthodox wedding. To everyone in our family, it was not his stepmother who walked her, it was his mother. That's not to disrespect Elana in any way. Akiva had nine years with Elana as a mother, but so far he has had 13 with Chana. Ask any of my kids who their mother is and their immediate response will be "Chana." After a moment's pause, they may modify that with more of an explanation about Elana, but Chana is very much their mother. And this is exactly what Elana would have wanted. She would have wanted her children to have a mother, not a stepmother. She would have wanted them to feel loved and cherished as only a mother can do. And she would have wanted them to love that mother back in exactly the same way. In Chana, Elana and I could not have asked for more. And my gratitude to Chana is impossible to express in words.

Coming back to Akiva's wedding, Chana initially felt insecure about walking Akiva to the *chuppah* with me (In Orthodox practice, both mother and father accompany a child down the aisle). As I've said, Chana has always been very comfortable with her role as the children's mother. But for some reason, when it came to this, she didn't feel right about taking Elana's place. Knowing how desperate Elana had been to play this role for her children, Chana felt that is was something that Elana had to do, not her. Whatever I would say to encourage her did not seem to help. In the end, she came up with a brilliant, albeit kind of obvious, idea. Let's ask Akiva.

Here's a paraphrase of what Akiva said to her. Mima, for so much of my life you have made me feel that I have a mother, a real mother. And I can't tell you how much that has meant to me. Now, on the happiest day of my life, you want to pull the rug out from underneath me and take that away?? He carried on, 'I am walking down the aisle with no one but you.'

For Chana there was no longer a question. Of course she would put Akiva before her own discomfort. More so, however, it taught her a valuable lesson. That God knows what is best and He decides who is right for a particular role. Who are we to think that we know who is the right person to walk a child down an aisle? We might create 'truths' in our own mind about what is right and what is wrong, what is appropriate and what is not, but ultimately God's plans are the ones that play out and they are always what they need to be. In this instance, God wanted Chana, not Elana, by Akiva's side on his wedding day and that was just perfect for him.

I see families sometimes where the role of a stepmother after the mother has passed away is a grey one. She is not the mother, but neither is she a stranger. She is in limbo and that creates uncertainty for the children and uncertainty for her also. In my mind, in a situation like this a family needs to keep the first mother firmly in the past and allow the new mother the space to provide the security and stability that the children require.

That does not mean to forget the birth mother or, God forbid, to disrespect her in any way. I hope that you have a sense from this book just how much love and respect I and our children retain for Elana. But Chana is our future, not Elana. It gives me a twinge of sadness to write that, but at the same time, I know that God does what is best and as our marriage goes forward I only see that more and more clearly.

Chana doesn't like me to thank her, so I won't. But I know it's not easy for her to have taken on all that she has taken on at a young age. She has eight children and has filled the shoes of a deeply respected, loved, and admired woman. Her greatest challenge of all, however, is the one she enjoys the most (at least so she says) — and that is being married to me!

Glossary

Amidah — the silent prayer recited three times a day (also called "*Shemoneh Esrei*")

Bas Yisrael — Jewish girl

Bitachon — trust in God

Bitul Torah — neglect of Torah study

BT — acronym for "*baal teshuvah*," one who returns to Judaism

Chad Gadya — Playful song

Chassidim — member of a strictly Orthodox Jewish sect

Chesed — kindness

Chuppah — the canopy under which a wedding ceremony takes place, or the wedding ceremony itself

FFB — acronym for "*frum* from birth," meaning one who was raised as a religious Jew

Gilgul neshamos — Kabbalistic concept of Reincarnation

Haggadah — Book which sets the order of the Seder and relates the story of Passover

Hashem — God; in this book 'God' and 'Hashem' are used interchangeably

Ima — mother, mommy

Kabbalist — A follower of *Kaballah*, the mystical teachings of Judaism

Kapparah — atonement

Kumzitz — a gathering around a bonfire

Madrich — counsellor, trainer or educator. (f.) *Madricha* (pl.) *Madrichot*

Midrash — rabbinic oral tradition in the form of stories

Mitzvos — good deeds

Pesach — Passover

Pirkei Avos — *Ethics of the Fathers*

Rabbanim — Rabbis

Rebbetzin — the wife of a rabbi; a woman of spiritual stature

Rosh Hashanah — Jewish New Year

Seder — First night of Passover

Semichah — rabbinic ordination

Shabbos — the Sabbath

Sheva berachos — the seven blessings recited at a wedding ceremony or the seven days of celebration following a wedding

Shiva — Seven day mourning period

Yeshiva — Orthodox Jewish college or seminary

Yissurin Shel Ahavah — troubles of love

Z"l — acronym for "*zichrono* (or *zichronah*) *levrachah*," may his (or her) memory be for a blessing